A Jackass at Every Turn!

A Jackass at Every Turn!

✦

How to Act Like an American When Everyone Around You Will Not!

Bear Brooks

iUniverse, Inc.
New York Lincoln Shanghai

A Jackass at Every Turn!
How to Act Like an American When Everyone Around You Will Not!

iUniverse books may be ordered through booksellers or by contacting:

iUniverse
2021 Pine Lake Road, Suite 100
Lincoln, NE 68512
www.iuniverse.com
1-800-Authors (1-800-288-4677)

ISBN-13: 978-0-595-36520-3 (pbk)
ISBN-13: 978-0-595-80954-7 (ebk)
ISBN-10: 0-595-36520-5 (pbk)
ISBN-10: 0-595-80954-5 (ebk)

Printed in the United States of America

This book is dedicated to my father, Jack Brooks Sr., who passed away in May 2004 from cancer. He was truly a great man in his own unique way. He worked for thirty-seven years at one company (unheard of these days). He was never rich with money but was rich with love and family, even if we did not understand when he was showing it. My father was one of those people that you would think was mean when you were young, but each year as you got older, started to understand what he was doing. He was stern in discipline but taught life's hard lessons well enough to save us from a lot of pain and aggravation. We could never leave the house without the phrase "wear a condom" attached as a good-bye. While the condom advice was well taken (I only have two children that I know about), we did not always listen to him on other issues and found out the hard way that he was right most of the time. We loved him very much and hope he is living the life in heaven he never got to really enjoy on earth.

Contents

Introduction ix

The Pork Barrels and Their Pork Bellies 1

Recessions Are Delusions Made Up by the Powerful. 21

The Law "Suits" 36

My God Can Beat Up Your God 42

"I Do Not Pay for Sex; I'm Married." (Yeah, Right!) 46

Practicing Medicine 69

The Anal Probe. 73

English: The "Mutt" of All Languages 77

Hyphenated Americanism. 83

Hey! Watch This 89

The Environ "Mental" ists 95

The Law of the Land: Well, It Used to Be. 98

Conclusion 105

Introduction

They are coming after you. You better be ready. The jackasses that run America are going to get you and hold you hostage. You will be a prisoner on the ignorance bandwagon unless you prepare yourself. The only way to prepare is by educating yourself. Good luck!

My main goal was to create a book that could be read by every American. I did not want to write a book full of lengthy words to impress anyone with my vocabulary skills. I only want everyone who reads this book to get the true meaning of what I'm trying to say. The one word you do need to know the meaning of is *ignorance*. Ignorance means you are uninformed or uneducated about a certain subject, not that you are a complete idiot.

I am no genius. I am not a scholar. I am not an English major. You may be smarter than I am, but I have one thing to say to that: *who cares!* I am just an average American trying to do my part to live my life the best way I can. This book is more of a list of my ramblings, opinions, and complaints about the everyday attack on Americans by every section of society.

Before we begin, I want you to know that this book is not going to be politically correct. If you are overly sensitive about anything (or everything in some cases), proceed with caution. If you are an open-minded person, then continue on. I hope you will get at least a few ideas or gain a different view on the things that go on around you in your everyday life.

The biggest crisis in America is that no one can admit when they screw up! If everyone in politics, media, education, and the like could admit when they screw up, America would be a greater place. Learn how to say, "I screwed up." Every problem has someone to blame. Stand up and admit it. You have to fix the problem, not find who is responsible. As they say, "Find the fault, not the blame." If we spent as much time fixing things as we do blaming each other, we could probably double our productivity. If you have already learned how to admit when you have screwed up, I salute you. I will be sure to make a toast to you while drinking my next daily twelve-pack.

Being an American does not mean you were born to a white, middle-class family. You can be and act like an American whether you are white, black, green, purple, or blue. Neither your race, religion, social standing, political views, nor anything else should affect your ability to love your country. I love living in America, and you should too. If you relocated to America and became a citizen, you should not be denied the rights that every natural-born American gets (other than the right to run for president). Remember one thing as we go forward: America, more importantly than anything, is a free country. *If* you hate it here, *get out!* There is nothing more than a passport and a plane ride standing in your way. If you want to change America and make it better, keep reading and working within our system to help change the problems. America is definitely not a perfect society. We have problems as does every other country.

It seems as if every time you turn your head, someone is either trying to steal from you or screw you over in some way. Usually, the daily attack involves someone taking money out of your pocket, but other times it is with so-called friends, relatives, or the like. You can be screwed at any moment; so you better look over your shoulder at all times. Be prepared for the inevitable, and be ready to fight back when needed.

Remember this: laws, rules, and major decisions in America are made by people who are usually so far out of touch with the average American that the rules they make do not even apply to us. Politicians and the like are usually from upper-middle-class or higher social standings. They know which fork to use with which meal course and which wine goes with meat and which with fish. You get the idea. They did not go through their childhood eating potpies with rice, TV dinners, and canned soup with grilled cheese sandwiches. They did not use outhouses like I did. They did not live paycheck to paycheck like I always have. They take their vacations in their second or third homes for eight weeks or more throughout the year. I have taken one vacation in ten years, and that was when I got married (my wife made me take one for our honeymoon). So look out for people campaigning for office who are out of touch, because, as soon as they are in office, they will do whatever it takes to stay there, including screwing you over to benefit the people who throw money at them. They will steal from one program and give to another to buy votes. If you want to see how stupid someone is, just give him or her a little power over other people's lives and watch them lose touch with the average person rather quickly. Politicians get what I call the "God syndrome" in which they think they are the omnipotent leader of the free world until the people wise up and vote them out of office. We need more people like Arnold Schwarzenegger. He is losing ungodly amounts of money by being the governor of California, so I seriously doubt he is doing it for the money. He gave up his salary to run California and helped with their budget problems. He will not be able to be bought (at least I don't think so).

I will not go into extreme detail on any of the issues in this book because it would take fifteen separate books to detail the ignorance and apathy of politicians in America. I will cover some of the most aggravating parts of certain topics and (when you are good and pissed off) let you investigate a little deeper if you so desire. I started this book with more than a hundred subjects and topics. Needless to say, I had to tone down my venting to keep this book within the attention spans of most people. If you do not like the flow of my chapters, get over it and keep reading. You might get lucky and learn something or at least get angry enough to get out and make a difference in our society. I am sure I have left out a lot of subjects, and the issues I mention may not be what you are interested in. You may not agree with me; you may think I am an idiot, and you have that right as an American. I will assure you of one thing: this book will make you *think* (if you can)!

Because we live in such a litigious (sue-happy) society, I have altered some of the names in this book to protect the *guilty!*

If you are one of those anal people (later chapter) who like to proofread everything you read, then get your pens ready. Get ready to draw "frowny faces" or whatever you do to make yourself happy. You will probably need more than one pen. Try to read this book and focus on the meaning, not the delivery.

Life is one big run-on sentence *and* so is this book, so let's get on with it.

The Pork Barrels and Their
Pork Bellies

This first chapter will be a little unsettling to a lot of people. These jackasses in the chapter title are the people who decided a long time ago that their ambition in life was to work for the good old U.S. government. I will briefly describe them and then give you a solution or at least a plan to prevent yourself from becoming a jackass too.

First and foremost is our esteemed Mr. Bill Clinton. We all know he received "special attention" from his intern while in the White House. I will be the first American to say this: *I do not care* whether Clinton received a BJ while he was president. Do you really think he is the first U.S. president to receive sexual favors from women? As with any powerful or public figure, you have to understand that women actually throw themselves at these men. Women have half the money and all the…Women have the greatest power in regards to having sex; they decide when it will happen and if it will happen. If a women wants to go out and have sex, all she has to do is go to a bar and pick any man from a group, look at his finger for a wedding band (single men are easier), and go for it. Unless she is butt ugly, odds are she will be going home with someone else. A man who brags to his buddies, "Hey guys, I'm going to get laid tonight," and goes to the same bar will come out alone and end up alone masturbating that same evening at home. If you believe that Clinton had to pursue this woman, then you are too naïve to vote anyway, and this book will not make any sense to you.

I think Clinton is a jackass because of the list of wrongdoings and lies he committed and because of the failures he achieved as our president. Whether you believe it or not, he deserves a personal life just like the rest of us; however, the rest of us, I hope, are not cheating on our wives. We all know that what he received was not "sex" though, because he said so. Mr. I-Got-Mine, Now-You-Get-Yours-Elsewhere has our little daughters and sons believing oral sex is not sex. We are now hearing reports of girls allowing boys to have anal sex with them because they believe that anal sex allows them to retain their virginity. What a crock! We did not need to spend millions just to prove he cheated on his wife; his lies and perjury are a different story. As for Clinton's political views, we see these failures come out of the woodwork on a weekly basis. The jury is still out on Mr. Bush.

Mrs. Clinton, on the other hand, will be running for president in 2008, and she will probably win. This woman stood by her man through sex scandals and a thousand other ridiculous issues while she was probably thinking, "What a jackass." She was just biting her tongue, waiting for her chance to jump into the spotlight. She did jump into the senate and, while still in office, signed and got advanced money on her book, all the while skirting the laws against public officials receiving money for book deals. She timed it just right, so that the deal wouldn't be sent to court. You have to understand that more than 50 percent of the population is female, and the majority of these women will put their beliefs aside just to see a woman in the White House. Add these women to the other ignorant party-line voters out there, and she will be a shoo-in. This will of course backfire in the long run, as they will soon find out this lady's plans for America. This woman wants America to be a Socialist society in which everyone relies on government for everything. She does not want Americans thinking for themselves or being responsible for their own actions. She wants the government to handle all health care, just like it does in other countries. She neglects to tell you that in these other countries it takes several months just to see a doctor for a routine procedure. Other countries have people dying because they cannot get the medical attention they need. She also neglects to tell you that her plan will not let you see the doctor you want. You will not be allowed to pay for a quicker service out of your own pocket because that would be antisocialist.

No one will tell you that we are paying more than $350,000 for Bill Clinton's office space in Harlem, New York. We will spend more on his office than we have for any other president in history. Not just a little more but a massive amount more. Does the mainstream media tell the general public that while Bill Clinton was president he told the Federal Aviation Administration (FAA) to treat any plane his wife was on like Air Force One? There is no telling how much it cost American taxpayers to hold airplanes and passengers at the airport gates while waiting on Mrs. Clinton.

I will get off the Clintons now, because it would take me several books to detail all their wrongdoings, including the ones we have not yet seen. Look over your shoulder. As we all know, the government is full of hypocrites and jackasses. So, we will continue on into the meat of the issues.

Lawmakers are jackasses. If the Constitution of the United States were written today, it would be more than 1,000 pages long. Maybe our forefathers needed the extra paper for the outhouse or something. First and foremost, why do we have so many laws? No human in the world could possibly attempt to learn even 10 percent of the laws on the books. How could the average American know and abide by them? There are more laws than there are people in some areas. It takes over a thousand pages of studies, claims, statements, and details to make one simple law. One set of laws overlaps others, some laws step on top of others, and some just completely contradict others. We do not need a different set of laws for every single level of government, all the way down to the sewer authority. Why can we not have one set of laws for Americans at the federal level and let the lower jurisdictions follow these and alter them to fit their particular situations? This way, if you have a federal law, it is still in effect in East Bumblefudge, New Jersey, or wherever you may live. A perfect example is the Alabama state Constitution that contradicts the U.S. Constitution in some areas. Ask Judge Moore about it.

Why are there so many stupid laws on the books? Who was the rocket scientist that came up with the law that you cannot have sex with corpses or dead animals? Is the general public that stupid? Laws also get in the way of common sense, as they did in the California forest fires. As soon as one of the forest fires started, there was a helicopter full of water within *five* minutes from the fire, at which point they had to turn back because of a law that says state choppers must be grounded at dusk. What a shame that a stupid regulation caused billions of dollars in damage to California. Lets go make some more laws.

Consider: oral sex is illegal with your spouse in some states. You are not allowed to have sex in a butcher's freezer. You cannot milk another person's cow. Liquor stores cannot sell milk. Drive-up ATMs must have Braille on them. You cannot drive blindfolded.

You cannot bathe two babies in the same tub. You cannot talk dirty during sex, and only the missionary position is legal. Men cannot wear gowns in some areas. You cannot shoot game animals from moving vehicles. The list goes to no end.

What makes members of Congress think it is just fine to give themselves a raise? With the economy in shambles, bankruptcies up, unemployment high, and everything in disarray, they find it a great time to raise their paychecks. I did not get a raise; did you? There are so many companies on the verge of bankruptcy, yet they are paying their CEOs millions of dollars in extra benefits. I will explain more of this in a later section. What part of economics did I miss? Do they think if you pay them more they will do a better job? This never works in the real world. Members of Congress must be *special!*

Political party affiliations are for jackasses. I will start this off by stating an unknown fact: the Democrats are not for the poor, and neither are the Republicans for the rich. Both parties have one goal in mind: to stay in power in any way they can. All laws, bills, actions, and other legal matters that politicians have wasted time on are slanted toward protecting their party. Every news article or report is slanted, so the facts favor their party whether or not it is true. Winning is everything to politicians.

Democrats are jackasses. They believe they are the only ones that know how to spend your money. The Democrats want everyone on welfare, Social Security, and other programs so that when everyone is reliant on the government, they will never lose power. They want to control your economic life but want you to have some control over your personal matters. Democrats want more environmental laws. They want no gay marriages, but they want gays to have the same rights as married couples. They want strong gun control. The party wants socialized, government-controlled health care. They want to hold hands with other countries preaching peace. They want abortion to be legal. They want education to be controlled by the government, to fail more children in the future. They want to keep the failure of a Social Security system. They want more people to be on welfare.

Republicans are jackasses. They do, however, want more self-reliance in economic matters, fewer taxes, and less self-control over your personal lives. The rich just happen to benefit as a result of lower taxes. Republicans want to be more self-sufficient with our environment and our natural resources. They are against gay marriage and benefits. They do not want more gun control. They want a free market system for health care. Republicans want a stronger military and a missile defense system to protect us. They are against abortion. They want to allow free choice in education and to strengthen discipline in schools with zero tolerance (which is a joke). They want to privatize the Social Security system and privatize welfare so churches will distribute money to the needy.

Libertarians want you to have freedom in both your economic and personal matters. To Libertarians, less government is more. They want the United States to responsibly get our own natural resources. They want gays to have the freedom to be so if they desire. They want no gun laws and a free market health-care system. They want to stay out of foreign affairs that do not pertain to America. They believe the government should stay out of the abortion debate. The Libertarians want to privatize education and the Social Security system. They also believe churches and individuals should be responsible to give money to the needy.

Most Americans have no idea which party they actually believe in. They believe what they hear on the news and other television shows. Before you decide which party you belong to, you need to research all the parties and all the issues and choose one that best fits your beliefs. Do not say you are a Democrat because your parents were; that is ignorant. Get on the Internet and see for yourself how you feel by taking the world's smallest political quiz (www.boortz.com is one location). This quiz is all over the Internet, and most people are surprised to find out they are actually Libertarian when they thought they were Democrat or Republican. Choosing a party used to come down to deciding between the lesser of two evils, but now you have a real choice, with several other parties to pick from. Good luck with whichever party you choose.

Wasteful spenders in the government are jackasses. I think before the government can spend any money on nonstandard issues, they should have to notify the public (in a well-publicized manner) of what they plan to do. Not that I would dare believe in mob rule, but public notification would give the people a chance to chew on their elected officials before such a vote could occur. A republic such as ours should not let our elected officials run rampant with our money without our knowledge. Why did a previous secretary of defense stay at the Beverly Hills Four Seasons Hotel at a cost of more than $10,000 to the American taxpayers? Such waste. I do not know how you feel, but I do not understand how we are spending millions of dollars studying the mating habits of brown bears or the life cycles of tree frogs, when we have other important issues facing America. Find somewhere else to blow it, or do away with these useless programs, and watch our budget get back in the black really quickly. If the government wants to blow money that badly, just send me $500,000, and I will tell you what tree frogs do. They are born, eat, sleep, sh*t, mate, and die…same as humans. Where is my money?

Consider this:

- $3.6 million was spent to create a wall to keep frogs from getting killed on the highway in Florida

- Another $3.6 million went to team building exercises for the postal service

- $1.8 million was spent to study how algae act in hot water

- $9.5 million went to fund studies on wood

- $170 million was spent to hand out condoms all over the world

- $4 million went to study shrimp

- $1 million went to study oysters

- $8.5 million went to study monk seals and sea turtles

Our Advanced Technology Program gives hundreds of millions of dollars away every year to the biggest corporations in America, such as IBM, GE, Ford, GM, and many others. Can you believe our government is giving tax dollars to the richest companies in America? See the Heritage Foundation (www.heritage.org) and Citizens Against Government Waste (www.cagw.org) for more details. When will this stupidity stop?

The basic financial concept is the same in any business (and that is what our government is): if you cut spending, you will increase the bottom line. Any amount you do not spend goes directly to the net profit column. Some politicians think a budget is an outline showing what *must* be spent. This is not the case. Budgets are guidelines on what you think it will cost to run a business. Just because you have budgeted to spend *x* amount of money on building and improving roads, that does not mean at the end of the fiscal year you go out and start repaving roads that do not need repaving (this is how it happens where I live) just to use all the money. We have roads full of potholes, a poor drainage system, poor street lighting, poor traffic control, and numerous other dangerous situations, and we find our wonderful government repaving a road that was fine just to spend the money.

The voting system is run by jackasses. Do you know why we cannot vote on the weekends? Voting on weekends would favor Republicans. Currently, the people most likely to get to the polls are retired people, unemployed people, government workers, and welfare recipients. These people are usually the ones coddled by Democrats. Democrats know that the typical Republican voter usually works on Tuesday or drives fifty miles to work and has a hard time getting to the polls. When you have businesses to run or jobs that really need you to be there, it is hard to take time off to vote. The lines are too long, the locations too few, and the system is in shambles no matter which way you look at it. As for the voting procedures such as hanging chads and so forth, if you are too stupid to figure out a polling booth, you need to be at home playing shuffleboard, or whatever it is you know how to do. Do not turn up after the results are not what you wanted and say you were disenfranchised or something stupid. The only thing keeping you from the polls is yourself or your eight children. Do not blame anyone else for not being able to vote. It is your responsibility.

Ignorant voters are jackasses. If you have no idea about the issues or the candidates, you need to stay at home. An ignorant vote cancels out a well-informed vote every time. This just puts the voting results on how many stupid people go to the polls. Let the people who know what is going on vote on the candidates.

Party-line voters are jackasses. If you go into the polls and vote straight down the line for either Democrats or Republicans, you are stupid. Stay home. Once again, you are canceling out someone else's well-informed vote. If you would look at the issues and the candidates, you would figure out that neither all Republicans nor all Democrats have all the answers. There are always cases in which a Republican voter finds that a Democratic candidate would do a much better job. A perfect example is Democratic Senator Zell Miller from Georgia. Republican voters vote for Miller over their own Republican candidate all the time. He is not afraid to go against the Democratic Party to stand up for what he believes in. This is something you never see in politics. You need to go into that polling booth and read the names of the candidates for each office. If you do not know either one of the candidates, do not vote on that office. All you are doing is supporting the failures of the voting system. We have intelligent voters going to the polls, knowing that their votes will not count but will just cancel out the ignorant votes. When someone tells you, "My vote won't count," tell them, "Yes, it will. It will cancel out a stupid vote."

Property rights abusers are jackasses. We hear too many cases of someone losing their land because some local government official decides that their land would be of better use belonging to a corporation or to themselves. Just as well, this program of eminent domain would not work with the masses. In some cases, we need to sell our property (at a fair market price) to the government. I do not think a corporation should be able to convince the local government that they would get more tax revenue if the corporation owned it. I do not think tax revenue should ever be the issue when trying to take someone's land. I can understand in the case of needing to build a new road to ease traffic congestion or a lake to build power generators due to population increases but never just to make more money. Big corporations can get their land the way everyone else does: overpay for it.

Anyone keeping our failing tax system in place is a jackass. The average American works over three months in one year to cover their yearly tax bill. I know taxes are a necessary evil, but we need to revamp this system *now!* The biggest problem is the politicians spawning ignorance among the voters. The people think a 10 percent tax cut across the board is giving something extra to the rich. This is stupid. 10 percent is 10 percent. A $400 tax refund means nothing to a millionaire, but it means a great deal to a normal working family of four. This is the same situation, only reversed. I do not know about you, but the tax refund check I received in 2003 helped me a great deal. I know the average American family does not make over $40,000 a year.

As with any other government plan, there are abuses within the system. A prime example: toll roads. Toll roads are supposed to take a tax burden off the citizens. The roads are supposed to take tolls until the road building is paid for, and then it reverts back to a normal road. This is not the case in any area I have seen. Someone figured out that they could keep charging tolls and use the money elsewhere to benefit them in another way. You hear stories of toll road money being used miles away to purchase land for other projects. Let the people keep their money.

Why are our tax laws thousands of pages long? Should it be that difficult to figure out that you make an income on wages, home sale profits, stock profits, or any other profit, and you should pay x percent of that income as taxes. Why does the average American need to pay (with money they do not have) for a tax professional to do tax paperwork? If you are like me, you do not have a thousand pages of tax documents. You probably have one W-2 form to fill out, a house, maybe two cars, and numerous children. It should be simple. There is too much room in the laws for cheaters and crooks to manipulate the system.

Don't tell anyone about the fair tax system because it makes too much sense. If you are unaware, there have been bills put in Congress to revamp our tax system with a fair tax plan. This tax plan would basically let you keep 100 percent of your paycheck. You would only pay taxes on items you've purchased. They are trying the fair tax system now in Iraq. The rate is set at only 15 percent. Ours is about 23 percent. The fair tax system would take the burden off of the companies producing goods. This would allow them to drop prices 20 to 30 percent because they would not have to pay taxes. Everyone would get a rebate check every month based on the size of their family to take the tax burden off the poor. You would not pay this tax on used items such as homes and cars. This system has many opponents, especially those in government who love to be in power. This 23 percent would cover the cost of all aspects of government, including Social Security and Medicare. See www.fairtax.org for more information. Neal Boortz and John Linder have a book about this plan, guaranteed to cure your ignorance on the issue.

The people in charge of our borders are jackasses. Our borders are our first line of defense against evil coming into our country. We should not have to worry every day about who is entering our country with drugs, weapons, or other illegal items. We have no enforcement at our borders. There are hundreds upon hundreds of miles of unguarded, ungated border along the Mexican border. The Canadian border is a joke too, but we have not had a vast amount of Canadians pouring into our country. In Mexico, we have hundreds of people dying every year while trying to cross the border in desert areas. If you are not aware, the desert gets blistering hot during the day and ice cold at night. In the southwestern United States, there are citizens leaving food and water out for Mexicans crossing the border so they will not die.

In California, the previous governor was attempting to give illegal aliens the right to a driver's license. The next logical step after this is the right to vote. Does anyone else see a problem with this? California already has a budget crisis, and the politicians in California want to start giving illegal aliens rights. This will be a never-ending program of giveaways that California cannot afford. The biggest reason for these programs is so that politicians can get illegal aliens to vote for them. I have no problem with anyone coming to America *legally*. Diversity is what makes this country great. We will never live in a perfect society in which everyone always gets along, but we can try to get along with one another.

The next argument is that illegal aliens contribute to our society. This may be the case, but illegal aliens do not contribute to the current tax system that will be supporting them with free health care and benefits. They may contribute to beer, wine, and cigarette sales, but they do not pay taxes. Legal aliens pay their taxes. Is this fair?

Illegal aliens work at places like construction sites, chicken-processing plants, and so forth that do not take taxes out of their paychecks because these organizations pay them in cash or personal checks. Is this fair to other Americans paying over 30 percent of their income in taxes? There is another argument against illegal aliens' work wages. They work below minimum wage laws, and this hurts other Americans trying to support their families. The minimum wage in America is far higher than what the majority of people in Mexico will ever earn. Some people will say these people with low-paying jobs in America should just get better educated so they will not have to compete with the illegal aliens; but that will never happen. The world will always be full of jobs that have to be performed cheaply. Manure will always have to be shoveled. If I had no job, I would be glad to shovel manure to put food on the table if I had to. When it comes down to it, there is no job in the world that is beneath you. You just have to work harder to keep yourself out of that situation.

The people in charge of foreign aid and policies are jackasses. This is a very aggravating issue to many Americans. The normal American, like myself, wonders every day why all of our tax money goes away to other countries. Even countries that hate us with a passion get millions of our dollars in aid and assistance. We have homeless and needy people in America, and we keep wasting money giving to other countries. I can understand helping to rebuild Iraq and Afghanistan. How many billions of dollars are wasted? How many homeless shelters could be built with that money? Just think, we could build a homeless motel with 200 to 300 rooms in every major city in the United States with all the money that is thrown away. The homeless people could work for the upkeep of the motels to earn their keep.

Another foreign-aid failure is our stupidity in selling weapons to other countries. How long will it take politicians to figure out that our own weapons keep getting used against us? Do they not understand that the Clinton administration sold major nuclear weapon and intelligence plans to China? Do they understand that this is going to bite us on the backside?

The people causing our jobs to be exported are jackasses. Large corporations do not open large offices overseas and directly offshore for the scenic ocean view. Large companies open offices elsewhere to cut down on taxes and over regulation by our government. We do not make it favorable for these companies to keep their offices, factories, and warehouses in America. Keep America employed first.

Whoever is really in charge of our public works system is a jackass. Only in America will you see people paving roads that do not need to be paved and leaving roads right beside them riddled with potholes. Roads are too narrow and prone to flooding, and there are numerous other problems; however, we continue to do unneeded work with too many workers. Look around you and think of all that we waste for a minute. I was on the road the other day, and I saw clusters of halogen lights on eighty-foot poles lighting the exit ramps and entrance ramps of a rural road thirty miles outside of Atlanta, Georgia. This is the only road on I-75 in the area with lighting of any kind. Not to mention that halogen lamps cost 50 percent more to operate than the traditional vapor lights. They are not just lighting the roadway but every foot of the entrance and exit ramps. They are powering over twenty-four halogen lamps per ramp (ninety-six lamps total) on a road that I have never seen a pedestrian go through.

Do road builders not understand that curves should be banked to the inside of the curve? Other countries seem to understand this strange concept. We have a great deal of road deaths every year because some rocket scientist figured we should build roads with curves that are flat or roll outward. How many more people have to die before they figure this out?

The people in charge of the prison system are jackasses. Why is more money spent to house a prisoner than some people live on in a year? We have people living on $12,000 a year, but the government figures it pays over $20,000 a year per prisoner. Where is all of this waste coming from? Maybe we should quit spoiling them with televisions, bodybuilding equipment, exercise mats, good food, or whatever makes their lives miserable. No one said prison was supposed to be a country club. If food costs are the problem, hire someone to bring the food in for cheaper. As for this ridiculous death row nonsense, I, along with the majority, want to know why it takes over a quarter century to put someone to death after a conviction. I think in an open-and-shut case, with very strong evidence, the death sentence should be carried out within a year. If you have proof on video or a mob of witnesses, and there is no doubt they committed the crime, kill them quickly. Brian Nichols, the judge killer from Atlanta, pleaded not guilty after shooting a judge, a court reporter, and two police officers. His case will take forever. Why? There is no question of his guilt or innocence. He is a murderer, and I think in this type of case, you skip the trial and go straight to the sentencing phase. It does not matter if he says he was insane or not. You do the crime, you do the time. There should be no reasoning to explain why he would commit this type of a crime. I personally do not care why he is crazy. He is a worthless piece of trash and needs to pay for his crimes. He needs to stand in front of the Atlanta police force and get shot in the stomach, slowly, time after time, until he dies. Shooting him in the head would be too quick and too painless. A year is more than enough time to exhaust any appeals and beg the governor for forgiveness. After that, you have to go!

Those in charge of making federal holidays are jackasses. We do not need a federal holiday every single time someone important dies. Government employees already have more days off during the year than do other Americans. Who do you think pays for all these holidays? That's right, you do!

We do not need to rename every road on the federal highway system after someone. Do we need to rename every hospital after someone? When I die, put my name on an urn and throw it in the ocean; that will be your tribute to me. Do the people who make these changes understand the costs to you and to every other taxpayer? Every business, person, and entity on that road has to get all new letterheads, envelopes, address stamps, bank records, checks, and not to mention business cards for all their employees. The business ultimately passes these costs onto you, in the form of higher prices for whatever product or service they are selling. If you get a chance take a look at the bills Congress is debating on, usually there will be over fifty different bills on renaming projects. What a colossal waste of time and money!

Am I the only person in America who thinks it is ridiculous to name an airport (Atlanta–Hartsfield) after a dead mayor, then try to rename it after another mayor dies? This is not the way it should be. What are you supposed to tell the grieving relatives of the person you are taking the legacy away from? Oh no, we were only renaming the airport after your husband for twenty years, then giving it to someone else. Did you know that after you are dead for twenty years, everything you are remembered for gets taken away? Some people seem to think so. It does not matter who was the greater person. I think it is disgraceful to dishonor someone in this manner.

The people looking after our inner cities are jackasses. How hard is it to pass a law that says if you own a building in the downtown area, you have to choose to keep it in good condition, sell it, or tear it down? Am I being simpleminded? I do not think so. We spend millions of dollars making laws with thousands of pages, but something this simple could be written on one sheet of paper. Make it the "clean it, junk it, or sell it" law. I ought to right laws for a living. One last note: you cannot rename a street infested with hookers and crime and make it sound sweet and innocent.

The war in the East is full of jackasses; none of which are the soldiers. To all you antiwar crybabies, you have to decide if you want to fight terrorism in the Middle–East, or do you want to fight them in downtown New York, Dallas, Los Angeles, or your hometown. Sometimes you have to stand up for yourself, and I believe we are doing that by not letting them scare us into submission.

Did you know our soldiers have to find their own way home after fighting for our country? They take them to an eastern U.S. airport, pat them on the ass, and say "See you in two weeks." I am one American who thinks this is just idiotic. Millions are spent on a single warhead, but nothing is spent to get the soldiers home to their families.

The Democratic Party is really making an ass of themselves in regards to the war. All we ever hear about is: where are the weapons of mass destruction (WMD)? Did any of the Democrats ever hear of the scorched-earth tactic in war that has been used for centuries to screw up the aggressors? When and if we do ever find WMD in Iraq, the Democrats or the liberal media will spin it into a new lie, saying that Bush staged it, and that we planted the weapons. Everyone knows he had WMD; he used them to murder thousands of northern Iraqi dissidents. Do you think Saddam Hussein is dumb enough to be caught with them? I don't. Hussein may be a nutcase dictator and murderer, but he is not stupid. Everyone in Iraq was so afraid of him that not one person, not one, voted against him in their election. You have to be pretty powerful and intelligent to screw a whole country over and smile while doing the screwing. It would have taken only *one* bullet to solve this situation, long before it escalated to this point. Someone decided years ago that U.S.-sponsored assassinations were illegal, but that does not mean someone else could not have performed this gift to society.

Does anyone in America know why all the European countries, such as France and Germany, hate us unless they need something or need someone to come to their rescue? France and Germany loved us during the World Wars but not now. Only until this terrorist war shows up on their soil, will they hate us. When the war on terrorism shows up in their countries, they will be squealing to the United States and the United Nations, "Help us, we love you!" Everyone you hear about in the news media shows hatred toward Americans. Whether it is out of jealousy, lack of freedom, tyranny, or whatever, these countries show hatred, most likely born out of ignorance. In eastern countries, the burning of the American flag seems to be a pastime. These countries preach hatred toward us, but their countries have thousands of our troops helping and protecting them. It seems to me that Germany is a second home to all the armed forces personnel. Everyone I know or have heard of in the armed forces has done their time in Germany. Why do we not get our troops out and let these countries fend for themselves? I think all our troops that are in countries that hate us would be better appreciated here in the United States, where they are needed more. Could we actually secure our borders with extra troops? No, that would make too much sense. I am not saying bring all the troops home but reduce the numbers according to each individual situation.

If the American people will think for a while about the issues in this book and act intelligently and not emotionally, we will still push for Republicans and Libertarians and still head uphill on this roller-coaster economy ride we have been riding in the past.

Recessions Are Delusions Made Up by the Powerful

Jackasses are everywhere. I do not know why an economy, as large as that of the United States, dances around one man: Alan Greenspan. This man decides whether the economy is going to run, walk, climb, or fall. The media, stock experts, Wall Street, and everyone else decide what they are going to do solely on what Mr. Greenspan says. I think he has performed well, but I do not think he should have complete control of the economy, like he is a big puppet master pulling the strings that make everyone dance. All the while, laughing about the power he possesses.

To the average American, a recession is something someone tells them about to make them afraid to use their own money. If Greenspan and the media did not preach "the sky is falling" mentality about recessions, there would not be one. The average American is not dabbling in the stock market. I venture to say that a majority of Americans do not have a great deal of retirement income saved. The average American could care less about what the stock market is doing. Most American families make less than $40,000 a year. If the media did not start these scare tactics about the economy, most citizens would go about life as usual: buying beer, wine, and cigarettes, and trying to survive the day-to-day issues facing them. Most people I know worry more about keeping their job, keeping their home, rearing their children, paying their bills, and keeping others from cheating us out of either. Only when the media starts the panic, do people start getting afraid to spend a dime. People stop buying or fixing up their cars and put their lives on hold until the media starts preaching that the sky is clear again. None of this would happen if it weren't for the frantic media.

Tax cuts are like defibrillators to the heart of a sick economy. Boy, do the Democrats hate this one. As with every other time in history, the Republicans gave money back to the people who really deserved it (the American taxpayer), the economy started turning around. Democrats think that only they know how to blow your money. Democrats always fight tax cuts by saying they will not work, but every time we have received tax cuts, the economy has improved. $400 to $800 is not a lot of money to some Americans, especially to the top 30 percent of income earners, but to the rest of us normal Americans, these tax cuts mean a great deal. Bill Gates makes $800 every time his eyes blink, so the tax cuts mean nothing to him, but tax cuts in the past have paid for my car, phone, and electricity bills for one month. I am broke, along with the majority of Americans.

Government lawyers are jackasses. All the way back to the 1800s, the economy has gone down the toilet every time the government sues a major corporation, and then miraculously rebounds as soon as the lawsuit stops. Why is that? Some examples are cases with Microsoft, CSX Railroad, Standard Oil, U.S. Steel Corporation, and many others. Whether they call it antitrust, monopolies or whatever, the government has pulled the economy down every time they have gone after these companies.

Job hunters are jackasses. When it comes to your livelihood, you should pay a little more attention to your appearance. If you come to my business with an earring in your nose, a tattoo on your head, ears pierced eight times, eyebrows shaved off, hair in a mullet, and you're speaking slang and just basically being a complete jackass, I will not hire you. Take this to heart. When it comes to the economy, the number one thing you can do to contribute is to have a career. Make sure you have enough pride in yourself to look clean, to speak clearly, and to want to make a good impression. If you are a slob in your appearance, you will probably be a slob in doing your job also. You do not have to be rich or have money to look decent at a job interview. If you do not have a suit, that is fine; as long as you look clean-cut. I have purchased complete suits at flea markets for $10. Remember to speak proper English when you are interviewing. Do not speak in slang terms. People make too many excuses when they do not get the job they applied for. They blame everyone else. It is not your skin color; it is not your education; it is not your job history; it is however, the impression you make when you go to the interview. I have given jobs to people who could barely speak English because they seemed aggressive and were willing to work. I did not even inquire about their education or their history.

When it comes to choosing a career, you had better do it while you are in high school, and you better think far into the future before making that decision. Too many college graduates are bartenders now because they did not plan ahead. Do your research. I wish someone had told me before I chose my career which jobs pay the best. Most people do not realize that a degree means nothing if there is no demand for that degree. Did you know we have garbage truck drivers where I live making over $60,000 a year? Auto mechanics can make over $100,000 a year, and auto body painters can make over $100,000 a year. These jobs may not be glamorous, but you tell this to a waiter at a restaurant making $25,000 a year with a college degree, and he will want to stab you. The best jobs are usually the ones no one tells you about until after you have made a different decision. The best-paying jobs for people without college degrees seem to be truck drivers, electricians, plumbers, construction managers, supervisors in mechanical companies, auto mechanics and painters, and home and business painters. These may not be the most glamorous jobs, but they pay the bills and will enable you to provide for your family. More jobs are detailed later in the education section.

Fraudulent people are jackasses. Keep your money in your pocket. Penis enlargement pills, fat tamers, weight loss schemes, and usually anything attached to an infomercial will not work well. If something works really well, it will travel across the country with blazing speed only by word of mouth. The problem is no one will regulate these scammers and make them prove their products work before they screw millions of people out of their money. When law enforcement usually goes after these crooks, it is often too late, and no one sees a dime of their money due to these scammer's lawyers.

Telemarketers fall into the jackass category also. They have some kind of radar that tells them the exact time I sit down for dinner or bathing my kids so they can call me to sell me some new type of udder cream, fat-control product, or exercise equipment to be used as a clothes rack in my home. Quit calling my house. I know why they call us. It's because a great deal of Americans buy all of this crap. This is why telemarketing is such a big business. Everything from insurance scams, long-distance plans, home siding, gutter salesmen, investment scams, and an unending list of crap *I do not need!* I think there is a right in the Bill of Rights stating I have the right to be left the hell alone! I swear I read that in there. Maybe that was just my very loose translation of one of the other rights. Hopefully, this new national "Do Not Call" list will work. As I was writing this book, the government was fining companies for violating this list. By the time this book is printed, the whole issue will be bogged down in the court system about someone's rights being violated, and someone will still be calling my house.

Bad CEOs are jackasses. I am no business genius, but it does not take a rocket scientist to understand you do not pay someone bonuses for running a company into the ground and doing an overall crappy job. Not in good old America though. We have the uncanny ability of paying CEOs millions while the company is on the edge of bankruptcy. Every business I have managed has a simple policy: you are either paid bonuses on sales or on net profit, usually the latter. Why is this a complicated procedure? Do you pay your kids bonuses for poor grades in school? "Good F, Johnny. Here's a fifty." With any small business, if you are not producing a profit, you can cancel Christmas for little Johnny and hope January is better. Corporate America, though, gives a CEO named John F. Cantrunabusiness a hefty million-dollar bonus.

Airline managers are jackasses. What other business is managed by morons? I do not know about you, but I am tired of my tax dollars bailing out businesses that run with no understanding of basic business economics. If you fly empty planes, you will lose money. Maybe with a new CEO, Delta Airlines can learn to quit doing stupid things. Delta actually brags that they fly thirty-two trips to New York every day. Why? These planes are not full. If someone is going anywhere on a plane and cannot wait an extra hour or so they need to get a new life. Fly the planes when they are full, or hold the flight a little while to consolidate passengers. Why is this hard to understand?

Investment specialists are jackasses. If you do not have time to spend all day worrying about your investments, stay away from purchasing stocks unless you have money to blow. The stock market game is played by people who live on insider information and are lucky enough to not get caught. Do you think Martha Stewart was a scapegoat because she is famous? I do. This kind of insider information happens every day. Did the media jump on the Democratic national chairman when he turned $100,000 into $18 million? No, but why? By the time you read, hear, or see anything about the stock market, you are too late. If you do not want to take chances with your money, put it in a money market account or a low expense mutual fund, such as TIAA-CREF. See www.clarkhoward.com on the Internet for a load of advice and self-help.

Welfare directors are jackasses. Government housing programs are a joke. Welfare recipients do not care. People in government housing have no pride in the homes they live in and do not appreciate the handouts they receive, that basically come out of every American's paycheck. I can understand people being down and out, but I cannot understand someone not appreciating or caring that they are getting something for nothing. Someone once proposed that people in government housing work eight hours a month to help cover costs, and the recipients thought this was an outrage. I think they should have to work twenty hours a week, but that will never happen. I see people all the time going into a store and buying two cases of beer, two bottles of wine, and then (with food stamps) throw ten pounds of meat on the counter. Buy beer and wine with your own cash, and buy meat with your food stamps? I think everyone receiving food stamps should have to go to a financial counselor to create a budget, and they should have to show records of trying to follow the budget next time they go to get food stamps.

Social Security is full of jackasses. Just a little information to those that do not know the facts because the government does not want you to know: *No one* was supposed to live long enough to receive Social Security when the plan was created. Now that our wonderful medical practitioners have allowed us to live a much longer life, what is the government doing now: raising the retirement age. Retirement payouts are not what has destroyed this system, but it's the corruption in the system. People who have never paid a dime into the system receive Social Security payments numbering in the millions of dollars. Systems fail when you keep adding more and more recipients. A true retirement plan was found in several counties in Texas, when they chose *not* to go with the Social Security plan but with a private plan. Now the retirees in those counties make more money in retirement than they ever made working. We need a new system and will never get one as long as the Democrats keep scaring the elderly into thinking they will lose all their money. The system pays out nothing as it is now, how many people thought that they could work for thirty-five to forty-five years and retire in poverty? The death benefit is less than $300. What a bargain!

You have the option now if you are younger to really make some retirement money, if you will just get involved *now* in a Roth IRA, a 401(k), or other retirement plan. The only decision you have to make on these is if you want to pay taxes on the money you put in (at today's tax rates) today, or the money you take out (taxed at 2040 rates). You choose which gamble you want to make. I believe I would rather pay taxes at today's rates with a Roth IRA, and when I retire, *all* the money is tax-free! Who knows how corrupt the government will be in another thirty-five years?

The consumer credit system is composed of no one but jackasses. No one, other than the IRS, has as much power over your life as the jackasses that run the credit bureaus. These people completely control your life, but do not have any responsibility for accuracy. When they screw up the burden is put back on you to find it, and then fight it for months. My brother has a credit rating that dates back to before he was born. His credit rating overlapped with my father's. The credit bureaus will do nothing for you except put the blame on the creditors and make them verify it. Just think, these people can keep you from getting a car, a house, or even a job and do not care about accuracy. Such power should not be given to any company without holding them fully accountable for errors. You cannot sue the credit bureaus.

As far as credit goes, there is only one thing that can repair credit: *time*. Do not make the mistake of not calling these creditors as soon as you know you are getting into trouble. You will be amazed at how many companies will work with you, if you are adult enough to call and let them know the situation. Too many people hide behind an answering machine, ducking and dodging calls from credit companies. They cannot kill you, so stand up and discuss this with them like an adult. You have to stop using credit cards. If you get in credit trouble, you need to create a budget, cut out wasteful spending, and follow your budget. Stay away from drink and snack machines. These machines will eat up your money faster than you can think about it. Start by sending extra payments on your higher interest, highest balance credit cards and the minimum payments on the rest.

Keep doing this until one card is paid off, then start working on one of the other cards. You have to get into a pay-it-off every month mentality to control your debt.

The most important thing you have to have to control your credit is a steady job. Credit is a great deal easier to maintain if you have a steady supply of income coming in. At some point in your life, you may find it necessary to file bankruptcy. Do not kill yourself over this. Work through it to get your life back on track. Remember, time is the only healer when it comes to credit. Do not let anyone scam you into thinking they can repair your credit for you. There is nothing a company can do for you that you cannot do for yourself. All they want to do is take your money. Do not let people tell you that credit counseling will not harm your credit; it will! They keep a credit scoring system, with less human involvement, and they do not care who you are or what kind of person you are. They look at these credit scores (in some cases a computer looks at the scores) and either accept or deny you at that time. Keep working on your credit, and time will repair it.

Banks are jackasses. I do not have a minimum balance of $10,000 in my bank accounts. This is the excuse the banks use to nickel-and-dime you to death. They charge you for every single thing they do. Banks have ATM fees, teller fees, check fees, monthly fees, and numerous others. They have the right to charge whatever they want for their services, but you, as a free American, have the right to take your money elsewhere. I got fed up with a bank with America in the name, because my bank charges would get over twenty dollars a month. I switched over to a credit union. I do not pay any fees other than ATM fees, which understandably help pay for the machines. They do deserve money for handling your electronic fund transfers.

They will let you bring in buckets of coins at a time and count them for you for free. My bank fees now are nothing, as long as I do not use another company's ATM. Credit unions provide the same services as banks for free, pay higher interest rates, have lower rates on loans, and will generally help you in person without acting as if you are bothering them. They make their money by keeping expenses down. This is the way it should be.

People who do not save money are jackasses. I do not care if you are at the poverty level; you need to have some money saved. I was down-and-out at a time in my life, living off of black-eyed peas with ketchup, salsa, and chips for dinner, and my spaghetti had to last for at least five days. I was in a very bad situation but luckily found a way to work myself out of that hole. It was very hard. If you are not saving now, you need to find some way of saving. Even a little money is better than nothing. The best way to save money is to have your savings taken out of your paycheck before you get it. The best savings plan for someone on a lower income is to do what I have done for years: *stop* using coins. I did this for years without actually knowing what I was doing. I would go to these evil snack machines and use dollars each time. I would get the change, and put it in my pocket. After walking around, the change would get on my nerves, so I would throw it in my desk. Turns out each time I would go to the store, I would never have change in my pocket; so I had to break a dollar any time I purchased something. Over a year's time, this change would add up to an amount between $500 and $800. This was not a great deal of money but has saved my butt many times over the last ten years. You can always go to the bank and get your money out, but it is a lot more difficult to sit down and roll coins for hours. This is just one method of making you leave the money alone. I eventually heard a more precise method of using this savings plan. The actual plan requires discipline, which I do not have. You have to never use coins, even if you have them in your pocket and force yourself to break a bill at every purchase. Some people say to do this with a $5 bill every time you purchase something, but I have never had enough money to stuff dollar bills into a jar.

Insurance companies are jackasses. The average American has never read any insurance policy they have, so you need to be prepared. Life insurance companies are betting you are going to live, and you are betting you are going to die. Life insurance for any working family is a must. The main thing you need from insurance is to protect your family in case you die. You want all your bills to be paid and your income to be replaced for at least three to five years. You want to purchase as much life insurance as you can afford. Do not get too much though, you might get bumped off just for the money. Read the fine print. You have to decide which type you want. Term is cheaper, but if you live twenty years, you can be without insurance and will have to start paying for another policy at higher rates due to your age. Whole-life is ridiculously high and after twenty years, you may get some of your money back, possibly with some interest. Then you start over. Some companies have term policies that will give you your money back after the term is over. These are harder to find but a great deal cheaper than whole-life insurance.

Health insurance is a joke. You have to either work for a massive company, or you pay through the nose for premiums. I work for a smaller company with fifty employees, and my part of the insurance premiums are over $600 a month. All you hear from the insurance companies are "group" policies; "group" meaning all the people you work with. This is a *scam*! I do work for a group; the group I call Americans. What about the group called every person you insure? We need to privatize health insurance, so that supply and demand will control the pricing on all sides. Someone needs to work for reforms of these companies. Otherwise, good old Hillary Clinton will get her socialist health care plan approved. Then I will have a new book to write.

In this day and age, you need property insurance also. Home and auto insurance plans both have their failures. You have to read every page of your policy to make sure you do not miss anything. Things they do not tell you will get you every time. Car owners find out the hard way, that they do not have rental car coverage on their policy. With automobiles being built like beer cans these days, it does not take a hard hit from another car to leave you without a car for three weeks. Hitting a deer can take weeks and cost $5000 to repair. It is a great deal cheaper to make sure you have this coverage. Home-owner's insurance policies do not always have replacement values listed that covers inflation on the items in your home and the costs to rebuild your home at today's prices. You will find out the hard way; when a tree falls on your home, and it rains, flooding all your personal belongings. You need to study your policy for any exclusion(s) that may come back and bite you. As for deductibles, most Americans do not have $1000 sitting around to spend every time a deer or dog jumps in your way. Some people preach raising your deductibles as high as you can. If you compare the premium costs, you would be amazed how cheap a $250 deductible is compared to a $500 or $1000 deductible. With the company I am with, a $750 difference in deductible would take over ten years in premiums to make up the savings. It does not take very bad luck to hit two deer in one year's time. With my luck the way it is, I am going for the cheaper deductible, betting that I am going to nail some poor non-domesticated (as the insurance companies call them) animal, while I am driving the rural roads. Do your research and comparisons to see if the higher deductibles are worth it, and figure how many years it will take for those premium savings to cover the difference of one accident. You will be surprised with the results.

Charities are one of the biggest groups of jackasses in America. If people actually knew where their money was going, they would probably stop giving altogether. Some charities actually care, but most do not. Do your research on the charities you give money to. Find out how much money actually goes to the cause they are begging for. You will be surprised to find that some charities do not get even 40 percent of the money to the actual cause. They are studying government plans on how to soak up all money taken in with politics, fees, salaries, and other wastes. How much of every dollar gets to the recipient? What about all the families of 9/11? While they sit around, certain charities were and still are taking in millions of dollars with *no* plans on how to distribute this money to the needy families. If my feelings are correct, I can tell you the majority of the people who died in New York on 9/11 did not have their finances in order. I bet they did not have their families covered with life insurance. If they did, the insurance companies were trying to weasel out of paying, stating the deaths were an act of terrorism or other policy exclusions. See the financial records of your favorite charity, and see if the director of the charity does not make over a million dollars a year. See what the other officers make. Charities are soaked with overpaid personnel and are overstaffed by unneeded people. Some reports state that only 20 percent of the money going to help needy children in Africa actually gets there. Look deeper into this before you give up your hard earned money. I would rather give some bum on the street my money than some charity crook. Why not just go to the liquor store and buy a case of Mad Dog to give away?

Televangelists are jackasses. Where do you think your money goes when you send it to these people? Fancy movie sets, high-dollar camera equipment, massive amounts of staff and employees to put on these weekly prayer movies. Choir members look like Liberace, everything on the set is solid oak, and tapestries galore. Show me one televangelist who is not a millionaire! What about the normal Americans on the edge of poverty sending in their money to these people because they feel guilty about not giving. I think I will just send Bill Gates a $20 bill so he can blow his nose with it. Nowhere in the world is there such a case as the poor giving so much to the rich voluntarily and not being forced to, such as with the government. Numbers are everything. Add up five million viewers sending in just one dollar each; see what happens with the amazing process of multiplication. Where is this money going?

Unions are jackasses. Unions are good for employees until they get too powerful. Funny thing about power, when you get some, you want more. Unions do look after their members, but when a union pushes too far, and the companies their members work for, go bankrupt, there is a problem. I have friends that preached the benefits of unions, until the day their companies locked their doors. Some wonderful unions did protect them though; they got to start over as rookies at other union controlled companies. Twenty-five years of seniority flushed down the toilet for the overpowering unions. Note the states in the North: homes cost 100 percent higher than do homes in the South. What is the point of driving the cost of living so high? People in the South can have a great home for $100,000, and the same home in Boston would cost $200,000. Is there a reason for this? Wages are higher in the North, and so is the cost of living. What is the point of *everything* being more expensive; it all equals out to about the same quality of living. Maybe it is just a numbers game that looks better on paper. Unions get stronger by sleeping with politicians and getting them on their payroll in the form of favors, perks and the like.

The Law "Suits"

The complete law system is full of jackasses. There are several things the average American cannot afford. Lawyers are one of them. Laws get in the way of common sense on a daily basis. People love to sue over anything and everything. The new word for a litigious person is a "sewer" because that is where they belong. Corruption is everywhere, and stupidity is running rampant, that is the wonderful American law system. Why do we have to have a system where we throw principles out the window? In our system of law, it is always cheaper for any company to pay off the plaintiff whether they are right or wrong. The justice system was set up to right the wrongs done to and by people. Somewhere along the way, the system became based solely on money. Who has it, and who does not is the basis of who gets a real defense attorney, and who gets a court appointed lawyer with fifty cases on him.

People also use the race card to jump into court to sue everyone. People who have a lawyer or who have a strong, easy-to-win case, get to go to court and steal whatever they want from whomever they want; honest people, who have been wronged, usually do nothing about their grievances (usually out of pride). I know a lady whose rights were violated by a very large company because she was pregnant and could not do anything about it because no lawyer would take the case on the facts alone. This person either had to pony up thousands of dollars for a retainer or go elsewhere. Needless to say, the person I speak of went broke and had to file bankruptcy due to the wrongdoing of this company. The honest people are usually left outside of the justice system in America.

As stated by Neal Boortz on WSB Radio (based in Atlanta), we need to go to a "loser pays" system of law, where the accuser would have to pay the defendant's legal fees if the accuser loses the case. This would wipe out half of the cases on the books, and all the fraudulent cases would magically disappear. No more greedy lawyers running the system. No more ambulance chasers.

Lawyers that propose stupid lawsuits are jackasses. Every time you turn your head, you hear of some new idiotic lawsuit coming out of the woodwork. Lawsuits against McDonald's because some stupid parents let their kid get fat. McDonald's did not make your kid fat. Shoveling crap down his or her throat without parenting made your kid fat. Fat is not hereditary as some people like to cry about. Fat is stacked on your heavy butt because you take in more than you burn. Do the math. Why do pickles burn your mouth when eating hot food? Because they are hot, stupid. Why does hot coffee burn when you are a stupid klutz and dump it in your lap? Because it is hot, stupid. Why does pizza burn the roof of your mouth? Because it is hot, stupid. Looking at all the idiotic product labels we now have in America will tell you how ridiculous the law system has become. New clothing irons say, "Do not iron clothes while wearing." All coffee cups must say, "Caution, hot contents," and spray paint says, "Do not spray in face." How dumb have we become to allow this nonsense to get out of control? If you hurt yourself doing something that would land you on "America's Stupidest Home Videos," then you should shut up, suck in your bottom lip, quit crying, and get a life. Judges should get a set of gonads and throw these cases out on a daily basis. There should be watch groups looking out for us, and every time they see a judge allow these lawsuits to go forward, we should be able to go in; throw the judge, the plaintiff, and his lawyer out the front door; and make them ride naked through town on donkeys (jackasses on jackasses). The average American does not understand that even though these companies were involved in these large lawsuits, the companies do not ultimately pay for the lawsuits; you do! Any company will pass on any expenses to their consumers in the form of higher prices. This is basic business economics that most people do not understand. Multi-billion dollar lawsuits, such as the tobacco settlements, do no more than fatten the wallets of the lawyers, and the tobacco companies pass the costs straight to the consumers. What a win against the tobacco companies. *No,* it is a shaft to the smoker!

Lawyers are jackasses because of the stupid questions they ask and the way they ask them. Lawyers start every question with "Is it not true that?" What law professor teaches this as a way to ask a question? What is wrong with "Did you?" I think it would be much simpler to understand if they would ask, "Did you have sex with _____ on December 11, 2003?" instead of "Is it not true that on the date of the 11th of December, in the year of 2003, that you did or did not have sexual relations with _____?" Being the average American, I would not know how to answer a question like that. I would not know whether he was asking me whether I did or did not sleep with whomever. By the time they got to the end of the question, I would have forgotten what they were asking me about anyway.

We hear of stupid questions filling the courtrooms all the time. "Were you alone or by yourself?" "Were you present when your picture was taken?" "Did he kill you?" "How many times have you committed suicide?" "You were there until the time you left, is that true?" "Are you qualified to give a urine sample?" These kinds of questions and many others are being dispensed by our lovely lawyers on a daily basis.

Lawyers are really good at putting words in your mouth and confusing jurors. If you could ask jurors about a trial and expect honest answers from them, you would find that most of the jurors do not understand the questioning process in the trial. The problem is that the juror would never give you an honest answer to keep from appearing stupid. I watch *Perry Mason* and get lost.

Due process is gone due to jackasses. Why does it take two months to go to court for a traffic ticket? By the time my court date comes around, I have forgotten about the ticket and would be going to jail for contempt. Why do murder cases take six months to a year when there are confessions, witnesses, and videos?

Civil rights laws are led by jackasses. The ACLU is a joke. Everyone gets his feelings hurt and his rights violated every time someone passes gas in America. Stop the nonsense! Nowhere in the U.S. Constitution does it say you have the right to not be offended and that your rights are above anyone else's. Every time anyone gets pulled over by the police for a traffic ticket, there have to be several police cars there to make sure no one gets accused of wrongdoing. Civil rights violation cases are the reason people get killed in police chases. People know that nothing can happen to them when they get pulled over. Police chases now take hours, cause thousands of dollars in damage, and endanger the lives of everyone on the road. I think this would stop if the police were allowed to beat the living hell out of the person when the chase is over. The criminals know nothing will happen when it's over; that is why they keep running. Our police have been castrated. Call me a barbaric idiot if you will, but I believe a great deal of crime would stop in America if there were such a thing as "punishment" following a crime. Terrorists get to sit joyfully in jail, being pampered, knowing they killed thousands of Americans. They know we will do *nothing*.

People skate out of crimes using Miranda rights. Anyone who lives in America has heard the Miranda rights on television. If you are too stupid to know you have the right to shut up and that, if you do not, the court will use your words against you, and the right to a free non-freeloader-paid lawyer before you talk with us, then you do not need to leave your home. The reading of these rights should not affect the outcome in any case. It is not legal to speed just because you did not get caught. Why would murder be legal because the police officer forgot to tell you not to speak? If you are guilty, you are guilty, no matter what the police officer does (aside from bashing your brains in to make you confess).

Racial profiling has solved thousands of police cases by narrowing down the amount of suspects. I can assure you some nun or a black man in a wheelchair did not blow up the airplanes and towers on 9/11. I have not heard of any twelve-year-old Caucasian boys in choir robes blowing themselves up in front of churches. Racial profiling has always been used and will always be used whether it hurts someone's feelings or not. It has to be done to help our police and armed forces do their jobs, which is to protect your right to be a big crybaby. Put some ice on it until the swelling goes down.

Church and state separatists are jackasses. Later in the "Anal Probe" section, you can read more on this. America was founded by God-fearing men and women who created the best country in the world with no real foundation to work on. They were led by the fear of God and used God in their daily work. If you do not want to say a prayer in school, do not say a prayer, but leave those that do want to pray alone. You do not have a right to the freedom from religion. Religion rules the world and will always run the world. Read a history book to cure your ignorance if you do not know the ups and downs of religion through thousands of years. Whether you are an atheist, a Muslim, a Baptist, a Catholic, or a dog-worshipper, you are not above anyone else. Do not cry when you see someone praying. Do you panic when a Muslim throws a rug on the ground toward Mecca to pray several times a day? Grow up, and keep reading the next chapter.

My God Can Beat Up Your God

The history of the world is based on which religion was reigning during that particular era. The average American, or anyone in the world for that matter, does not know any part of religious history. Almost always throughout history, religion was forced upon the people by whichever tyrant had conquered that region at that particular time.

The Sumerians, the Egyptians, the Assyrians, the Babylonians, the Hittites, the Greeks, the Persians, the Romans, and the Ottomans all took over at different times in history, and whether the people believed in religion or not, they were forced to follow the religion. The religious either had to take it or risk being massacred. The earliest religions worshipped gods, such as the god of storms, the sky goddess, the sun god, Zeus, Poseidon, Amon, Osirus, and many others. Other religions such as Judaism, Hinduism, Buddhism, Christianity, Roman Catholicism, Islam, and others started themes of monotheism (the belief in one god). Judaism, Christianity, and Islam were all based on the belief in the prophet Abraham and were based in some form on the sixty-six books of the Bible, which were written at different times by different people.

Most religious leaders are jackasses. They have failed their followers in numerous ways. Some leaders are in it for the power, some for the money, and some actually for their religious beliefs. I have always said, "Show me a poor preacher, and I will show you some-one who actually cares about God!" Religious leaders in America live in homes paid for by their congregations. They do not pay taxes. Their church provides them with everything, and then it pays them a salary on top of that. I have never met a preacher that did not make a lot more money than the average American. Preachers always live better than their parishioners.

Religious people who push themselves on others are jackasses. One day in my lifetime I would love to talk to a preacher or member of a church that did not add, "Why don't you come to our church Sunday?" My religious beliefs are not yours, my religion may not be yours, and I am not converting to your religion, so leave me alone. You will know if I want to join or visit your church the day I show up at your door. Do not show up on my doorstep trying to push your religion on me. Door-to-door religious marketing aggravates everyone I know. Why do you persist? Are you taking the peaceful approach to forcing your religion on others? If you want to push your religion on others, you had better know the history of your religion. The conquests, the evil, and the wrongdoings that have been performed by your religion need to be known before you spread it. Tell the truth. We all know that no religion is perfect. Learn for yourself.

Sex offenders in the church are jackasses. The leaders cover these accusations up until someone calls them out. When called out, all they do is move these offenders to another area. In the real world, they would be going to prison for life to become some large, hairy man's boyfriend. When the church is involved, however, this will never be the case. These perverts could not survive in the real world.

Peace hating religions are jackasses. What God, in any religion wants people to kill themselves and others, with bombs strapped to their bodies? These religions have failed their people by not teaching them the history of their religions or the history of the countries they live in. The Palestinians and Israelis do not know their own histories. The leaders fill children's heads with lies, and when they are teenagers, they are full of hatred toward one another.

People have not been told the truth when it comes to the Israeli-Palestinian conflicts. This conflict is mainly based on one thing: the Arabs hate the Jews. Palestine was never an Arab country or a major city. Read your history books. Moses was said to have brought the Hebrews to Palestine somewhere between 1300 and 1500 BC, depending on the book you read. The Jews were the only people to use Palestine as an important area. People do not know that until the World War, the Israeli and Palestine areas were still a part of the Ottoman Empire. The borders were set up after the war trying to appease everyone but could not. The whole issue of children blowing themselves up for Palestine is ridiculous. If you do not understand the conflict, read an unbiased account of history, which most Arabs cannot obtain in their countries. There is a reason why most countries in the Middle East still will not allow television shows other than what is government sponsored. The governments want their people to continue being ignorant.

People do not know that the religion of Islam started out as a peaceful, open-minded religion. Mohammed knew people would not follow his new religion if they knew how abusive it would eventually become. When he started, he wrote that Mecca was the center of Islam, even though the people in Mecca did not want him there. He settled in Medina to gather a following. He eventually took over

Mecca by force, murdering everyone there. He also took over Palestine and Jerusalem by force. This is the best way to spread your religion, I guess, because this was how it has been done throughout history. Some religions have spread peacefully, but I do not know which ones.

"I Do Not Pay for Sex; I'm Married." (Yeah, Right!)

Family and money are two of the most important things in my life; do not screw around with either of them! There are many issues regarding your family and home life that you have to deal with on a daily basis. You have to be on alert; due to the number of ways people can attack you and your wallet at home. I will discuss many different areas of home life, including both married and single people, because everyone has things they need to improve.

Dating is for jackasses. Most people go through their early dating years being shy and withdrawn. There are many factors that cause this. Sometimes, it is the fear of rejection; for others, it is the fear of commitment. For those shy people, you need to just jump in head-first and ask the other person out. All you have to lose is your pride if you get rejected. You will usually get rejected, so if you get out there and get a few out of the way, it will toughen you up. The fear and hurt feelings go away, and you will have more confidence the next time. All the other person can do is say, "No," but they could surprise you and say, "Yes."

Do not try to go to bars to find your future wife (if you're looking for sex, that's different). If you find your wife at a bar, you will probably find out later that she will go to bars without you when you are married. Some people are lucky and find their wives in bars and live happily ever after, but these cases are definitely not the majority. Do not go looking for a spouse! Let it just happen. Do not put pressure on someone to commit to you, or it will backfire.

Dating costs a great deal of money. Try to find ways to have fun with a date that will not eat up your paycheck. Go on nature walks, go to parks, have a picnic, etc., to keep costs down. When I was dating, every date would eat me alive with movies, dinner, drinks, popcorn, candy, and the giant list of overpriced things you will be paying for. I am not saying take her to Krystal's for dinner, but be aware of your budget. I know of people who would not have money to eat lunch for the next week because they used their all their money trying to impress women on Friday and Saturday of the previous week. If you have to impress the person you are pursuing, then you need to stop and rethink your goals. I have had women that wanted me to spend money on them, and it backfired every time. I did not have money for dating. My best dates involved a woman coming to my apartment, renting a movie, ordering pizza, and making a few mixed drinks; the entire evening cost about $20 to $25. You cannot have a few drinks at a bar for that price.

Dating is emotionally draining. Each person has to contend with questions of adequacy. How was the other person's sex life before me? How do I compare to the previous partner? Am I funny enough? Endowed enough? Am I too fat? These and thousands of other questions bounce around in your head. All I can tell you is if you want to be happy, you will have to go through many dates, many emotional roller-coasters, and a vast amount of money before you find someone who will put up with your quirks and issues. This is the key to a happy relationship: finding someone that will put up with you. Most people can change very little when it comes to relationships. Do not ever think you can find a supermodel who is a bitch and turn her into June Cleaver. It will never happen.

Men, you have to remember one thing: women have 100 percent of the power when it comes to dating. They decide when, where, if, and for how long you are going to date. You decide how much money is in your wallet (and bank account). Men always act like they are studs to their buddies when they first start to date a women, but every man that has been married knows the single guy is always full of sh*t. Everything a single guy says about first dates with new women are usually false. If anything he says sounds like bragging, he is lying. Guys will say they have this new girl wrapped around their finger, or that they have the greatest sex in the world. Ask the woman, and you will find the truth.

Married people are jackasses. Marriage is like a hot sex dream: both are better when you are asleep! Single people cannot even begin to understand the ups and downs of being married. You may be shacked-up with someone, but believe me, it is *not* the same as being married. "Money isn't everything" is what we hear all the time (from people who haven't got any). Well I've got news for you: it is, when it comes to getting married, having children, and living a normal life. To be a good spouse and a parent means having a good job and a steady income; this is the most important thing you must have. If you do not have a steady job and income, you need to stay single, unless you are marrying into money. You need to live well beneath what you can afford. You need to buy a house for $20,000 less than you think you can afford. Do not try to impress people with your vehicle. I sold a $35,000 truck and bought myself a 1986 Toyota 4Runner to save money. I know what sacrifice is.

Marriage is a huge sacrifice in every aspect of your life (if you want to stay married). You had better be emotionally stable and happy with yourself *before* you get married. A marriage is emotionally draining. You have to be willing to think of yourself last when it comes to marriage and to your children. If you cannot do this, you need to marry your hand or personal massager. Women have mood swings; men have mood swings, and both will make each partner want to kill each other. Do not think you can go to bed mad either because you will both wake up mad, and the fight (which was probably pointless to begin with) will continue on into the next day. In most cases these days, people find that they cannot get along and end up getting divorced.

Divorced people are jackasses. Some people are professionals at divorce, and I am not talking about the therapists. If you have been divorced two or more times, you may want to think about yourself first, then think about what you are looking for in a spouse. If you have been divorced multiple times, you may want to think back and decide if you actually put your spouse's wants and needs in front of your own. If you know you did all you can and you put your spouse's needs first, then you may want to change the standards you are looking for. If you keep looking for a supermodel, that is what you will get. Most women are not supermodels, and from what I have seen, the best wives and mothers are attractive but are not supermodels. If you are a woman looking for a "hunk," you will find one, but you will soon know what he is a "hunk" of. Attractiveness goes hand in hand with shallowness. Try to find someone you are compatible with, and I do not mean just sexually. Any two jackasses can have sex and dumb-asses breed new dumb-asses.

The divorce law system is nothing but jackasses. Everyone knows some man who has been trounced in the courts when it comes to divorce, alimony, and child support. I personally know several men who have been screwed hard by the system. I know one man who has to pay $1,200 a month to his ex-wife for child support, when he only brings home $1,800 a month after taxes. He has to live with his parents; otherwise, he would have to go on welfare to be able to live. Great system. Another friend has an ex-wife getting $1,800 a month, and the wife always made more than $75,000 a year by herself; the husband makes around $50,000. Now the wife gets an additional $21,600 a year, and do you think she spends any of this money on the children? Fat chance. This system has failed miserably. I can understand deadbeat dads needing to be hunted down and publicly humiliated, but this divorce system needs to be changed. I could not pay my wife $1,200 to $1,800 a month in support; it would be cheaper to kill her.

Parents are jackasses. Do your children a favor *before* you have them, and get prepared. You have to be prepared to put your life on hold for a minimum of three years, from the time your children are born, before you can start to resume any type of normal life. If you cannot stop your partying, drinking, going to the movies, and having fun, then you had better not have children (unless you want to be another sorry ass parent). You will not have a social life to speak of. You do not need to dump your kids off with everyone else so you can go out and party. My wife and I have been out to eat *one* time, in 2003, and that was our anniversary. The remainder of the time, we are full-time babysitters. We have two careers and two children. The best times of my life.

Children are expensive. Before you get the little vomit-poop machine home, your bank account starts going down. Car seats, cribs, formula, diapers (by the hundreds), drugs, doctors, clothes, and last but not least, toys. If you do not have a good job with a steady income, do society and yourselves a favor, and keep it in your pants or wear a condom (if you know how). Kids have a great way of bringing out the greed in other parents. Parents of other children will send you invitations to their children's birthday parties to get a gift from you but will never show up at your children's birthday parties. When you have children, for some reason, your electric bill, gas bill, water bill, and food bill start to climb. It seems as though the taller the children get, the higher your bills get. Every light in your home will soon be left on; every television in the house will stay on, and the washer, and dryer never seem to stop.

Children are emotionally draining. God makes children cute to keep you from killing them. Children will push every nerve in your body, until you are ready to snap. You will soon learn how to step back and count to ten to settle your nerves. If you have had children and have not divorced yet, you will need to learn to take turns leaving the house for several hours at a time to keep your sanity. Children are very stressful. You will never be able to sleep soundly again. The whining never stops. They fight constantly with each other. Children have an amazing way of going deaf every time you call their names.

Children need guidance when it comes to feeding. When children are young, you have to feed them whatever they will eat. My son lived on peanut butter and milk for the longest time because that was all he would eat. After attempting other foods thousands of times, we were able to get him to start eating normal food. It was a slow process, but we kept trying, and now it is working. My daughter on the other hand, is a pig. She would eat a cockroach if you put it in front of her. We had to limit her intake and water down her milk so that she would not get fat. Feeding children is the biggest child rearing problem we have with our society. People always try to blame someone or something, when they themselves are to blame for letting their children become fat slobs. It is never the parents' fault; they try to sue McDonald's because they sell fattening foods. The judges in that case should be punished along with the parents for blatant stupidity. Other parents try to blame genetics, but not the five pounds of ice cream and candy they stuff down their children's throats on a weekly basis. People, stop feeding your children crap. You are to blame for your child's health and well being. If you super size your child's food, you will be super sizing their fat bodies at the same time.

You as a parent are responsible for your child's actions. Discipline has disappeared in American society. Long gone are the days of schools paddling badly behaved students, children having to walk to get their own switches (as I always had to do), and getting beaten with wooden spoons. Today there is time-out. Wow, what a concept. We now have thousands of self-help books written by people who either did not have children, or they had the money to have their children reared by nannies or someone else but themselves. Most parents I know who have tried these "gentler" methods have failed their children. Children have to know right from wrong, and this lesson must start at a very early age. After a child reaches school-age, it is almost impossible to repair the harm you have done to your child's idea of discipline. Children need to understand that "no" and "stop" mean to stop in their tracks and look at you. Also if you call a child's name, they should stop and look at you. There have been too many cases of children running away from their parents in a crowd and disappearing, or a child running away from their parents' calls and getting run over by a passing car because the child would not acknowledge the parent calling them. Both parents must take an active role in the consistent disciplining of their children. You definitely do not want your home to be a case of good-cop/bad-cop, or you will both want to kill each other.

You, as a parent are responsible for giving your child an education. You need to start planning (before the child enters school) for their college education. If you start a 529 plan early enough, you would not have to save that much to help cover the child's education in any public college. Your child may get a scholarship, but do not rely on that eighteen years from now. Georgia has a Hope Scholarship program (funded with the state lottery) for all children with a B average, but it will fail long before any of your children get to high school. Teachers feel guilty now about holding children back, so they give Bs to failing students. So the logical result (with thousands getting scholarships they do not deserve) is the Hope program will be bankrupt within ten years. What a shame for the deserving students, but it is okay as long as the teachers do not feel guilty!

If you can in any way do this, you need to get your children into private school as soon as you can. Hopefully, we will have a voucher system soon that will allow your child to escape the grasp of our worthless government school systems. These schools are failing our children left and right. The teachers are underpaid. The schools are overcrowded within a few years of being built because of pathetic planning agencies. The only thing government schools are good for is trying to get your child hooked on Ritalin or some other brain-deadening drug. How did children survive hundreds of years of education without these wonderful mind-altering drugs? The reason for this is that lately teachers do not want to deal with a child that needs to be given brain stimulation in school. They want your poor child to sit in class like a zombie and listen without commotion. Children that act bored in school, usually are, and they need to be taught subjects using more stimulating methods. These students are some of the brightest in school once they have received some type of stimulation, either through making learning fun, or the teacher uses another method besides regurgitating (throwing up) information from a book.

A child needs to learn the meaning of saving money as soon as they can count and understand what money is. I did not learn until later in life, and it was too late. Children need to learn to save a minimum of 10 to 20 percent of all the money they make or receive as gifts. I am teaching my children to save 10 percent of their money for short-term goals and another 10 percent for long-term goals. If your child can learn this lesson early in their life, they will never have a problem buying a car or a house, and they will always be prepared for the inevitable financial disaster that we all go through. I never prepared a "rainy day" fund and have regretted it every time I have to repair something unexpected.

The department of family and children services is a giant group of jackasses. As one of the biggest failures ever invented, this program needs to be completely revamped. The system is completely understaffed by irresponsible people, who have no possible method of protecting children. The abuses of power they use are reported daily. The negligence reports are too numerous to list. Children die repeatedly, who are supposed to be in the department's care. They repeatedly try to take children from good homes just because a child broke a bone or got bruised just being a kid. If you have a 2-or 3-year-old without bruised legs, skinned knees, and black eyes, you obviously did not let the kid act like a kid does, uncontrollable. While family and child care officials are going to hospitals searching for hurt children, other children are dying by being left in cars by unfit parents. If you want to find a bad parent, all you have to do is go to the grocery stores or the liquor stores, and look for children that have been left in the parent's cars. This is a direct sign that the parent does not care for the well-being of his or her child. I have never and will never leave my children unattended in a vehicle for even a second. The courts and the system have long failed our children. Children involved in divorces are repeatedly given to the least loving of the two parents, just because a certain law says it must be done that way. I would rather have a child be with a poor, loving mother than a rich, careless father and vice-versa.

Anyone involved in real estate is a jackass. Look out: sellers, agents, brokers, and financiers are all after you. There are many things you need to know before buying a home. Whether new or used, they all have problems. I will go over a few of those problems, and I hope they help you in some way.

Whether you are buying a new home or a used home, the most important thing you can do is to see this home during a rainstorm. It may be a pain in the butt, but the regrets you will save are well worth it. I found out the hard way that drainage is one of the biggest problems a homeowner will ever face. Rainwater has a way of finding its way downhill; it goes around, through, or over whatever it sees fit to find its way to the lowest point in any area. Water will destroy a home, the yard, and anything in its path; it will even dig trenches and make canyons in your property. I, along with my neighbors, found this out the hard way, as we were outside in torrential downpours, clearing paths for water to run down drains and through our yards. My next-door neighbor has the beginnings of another Grand Canyon starting in her yard. I was lucky; I only have to get my ark out when it rains to get through my yard.

You need to go through the house yourself to inspect insulation, check for curved walls, make sure they put all the wood siding on the house (not just insulation board over studs), and numerous other screw ups before you actually sign any papers. If you are building a new home, you need to inspect it regularly for mistakes. I went every few days, and I missed a great deal of mistakes that did not turn up until years later. In new homes, you want to make sure they put all the electrical outlets in, all the outdoor lighting is correct, and that you have running water and plumbing that lead to the outdoor faucets. Make sure the house plans do not change as you go along. My builder tried to give me sheet-rocked walls, when I was supposed to get spindle railings on the stairs. I was supposed to get three large radius windows put in the back wall of my home, and the framers completely missed it. These kinds of problems are a much easier to fix if you catch them early. Make sure your builder does not bury scraps in your yard, or you will have mystery holes the size of automobiles appearing in your landscape. Also make sure (unless you want a red brick lawn) that your builder does not scrape all your topsoil off the ground and sell it.

In older homes, you need to inspect for termites, roaches, and ant trails that may lead to problems later on. Check all the crawl spaces for any signs of damage and for leakage of any kind on walls and framework. Check the gutters for clogging and overfilling because overfilled gutter water usually finds its way into the walls and roofs of older homes.

First and foremost, you need to get your credit reports from all three bureaus. Correct all the errors that *will* be there. You will need to research financing options and rates with several lenders before you sign anything. It is amazing what one percentage point can do to your total loan payback over thirty years.

You need to research area prices for the same types of homes, for new and used homes. A home less than ten miles away from mine and built by the same builder is over 50 percent higher. Both homes were built in similar subdivisions. If you have never owned a home, you need to go to a football stadium and run up and down the bleachers one-hundred times before you make this decision. Buy a ranch home. Stairs only look good on television and are fine if you never do work around the home or never have to move furniture yourself. Stairs will kill your children. Stairs will kill your grandparents or other people who get drunk at your home. Then we will have to write a chapter on liability insurance fraud. Do yourself a great favor and think long and hard about having stairs in the home. I regret this every day of my life. I am a young man and hate having to go up and down the stairs five times to get tools to fix a door or anything else.

Home repair and improvement contractors are jackasses. You need to start saving the day you move into your home for the inevitable repairs! I made the mistake of being able to build a home inside and out myself. I unwittingly thought my home repair skills were an asset when we moved in. Boy, was I wrong. Whether your home is new or used, after five years, you will have to have things repaired or upgraded. Hopefully, you do not have to pay the outrageous prices to have someone repair anything for you. If you do, you need to shop around; you will be amazed at the different prices you will get from different companies doing the same job. Home repairs are not like auto body repair rates, which are regulated and dictated by computer programs. Any person with a truck and a ladder can call himself a handyman and knock on your door. You need to make sure the person is insured and bonded before letting them touch your home. There is nothing better than having someone falling off your roof and breaking a bone to get this life lesson.

As for my home, my wife has painted some rooms five times in the six years we have lived there. We bought our home brand new, and I think we have already rebuilt it at least one time on our own. It would have been cheaper to tear it down and start over. We have remodeled floors, decks, fences, walls, cabinets, fixtures, and everything else in our home. I hope your spouse is house-stupid when it comes to decorating. Do not let your spouse watch *any* home improvement shows on television, or your "honey-do" list will never end. I have twenty projects yet to be finished because the new projects keep overlapping the old ones.

Jackasses control your computer. One thing I want you to know about computers is that computers *do not* make mistakes. Do not blame your computer every time you lose a file. Computers only do what they are told. The failure may not have been your fault, but it definitely was the fault of some human. A human programs every function a computer does; therefore, any malfunction (aside from complete shut down) was a screw-up by some human along the line. Any normal American will never master a computer. We slug along hoping we will not cause catastrophic failure in the system and hope our hours of hard work do not disappear.

Using chat rooms and message boards is a major sign that you need to get something better to fill up your time. Unless you work on computers all the time in your business, I suggest you stay away from these areas. It will only be a matter of time before someone is after you for child molestation or something stupid like that. Mr. Michael Jackson, the singer, probably used these to coerce children. If you want to talk to people, get a phone. Everyone I know can run that hole in their face a lot faster than anyone can type.

Pop-up ads and porn sites will eventually destroy the Internet. Do not push your porn sites on me. I know where to get my porn. I'm a man; I understand porn. Men are drawn to women they cannot have or will never get. Porn shows a man what his life will never be, except for that night where he drank too many tequila shots with his cousin. Porn sites pop up now while you are surfing innocent sites for real information. As Neal Boortz said, "Do not look for 'leather whip'," or you will have to shut your computer down to stop the pop-up porn sites. Just like telemarketing, there is a reason for the pop-up ads; somebody keeps responding to them. If all you have time to do is use message boards and chat rooms, you need to get a life, or at least a dog.

So-called friends are jackasses. You want to know who your friends are? Tell somebody you are moving and see how fast your friends suddenly have to go out of town or become busy. Friends have a funny way of loving you while you are having a cookout with plenty of food and booze. I have several friends, but they never come around because I am always working on my "honey-do list." I have helped every one of my friends and relatives move their crap from their homes several times. When I moved into our home, I had my wife, a female friend, and myself moving an entire home. It was just hilarious watching us move large furniture, heavy boxes, washer/dryer, and televisions. All I can do is laugh, just thinking how stupid we looked struggling with all the heavy items. One hernia and two hysterectomies later, we got everything moved in. We still have not unpacked everything. Unpacking just keeps getting pushed further down my "honey-do" list.

Neighbors are jackasses. I want to kill your dogs for barking. How many times does your dog have to be run over by an automobile, before you put it in a pen or a fence in your damn yard? Who told you to feed the stray cats? Now I have to open the hood to my vehicle every morning when it is cold outside, so that I do not make cat puree before I go to work. What a hassle. Cut down your damn trees so they stop falling on my fence. Why do you let your three-year-old kids play in the street unsupervised? Did you not see *Pet Sematary*? Children are not as replaceable as dogs are, idiot!

Enemies are jackasses. You know the type; there is always someone who loves to start a fight (usually about nothing). It takes a man to walk away from some jackass trying to get under your skin. You have to be able to walk away, even if the other person is wrong. I know people who have been fighting for years over nothing because both of them are too full of stupid pride to walk away, and let the other person win. Learn how to stand up for yourself by walking away, and you will be a lot happier in the long run.

Drivers are jackasses. People cannot drive without any distractions, much less when they are eating or talking on the cell phone. There is no excuse for the number of accidents that have been caused by such things. If you cannot walk and chew gum at the same time, what makes you think you can drive and talk on a damn cell phone. Pull over and talk if you cannot pay attention to your driving. Do not put on your makeup (especially the eyeliner), while you are driving.

Just a note to you ignorant drivers who think higher-octane gasoline is cleaner; it is *not*! All gasoline is regulated and is just as clean as any others. Higher octane ratings are only needed in high performance, high compression engines. If you want to be sure to get good gasoline, go to a station that sells a lot of gas, this will lessen the chance that you will get water or contamination in the fuel. Why do people try so damn hard to get the fuel pump to stop on the exact dollar amount? People try to stop the pump on exactly $10 and then go in the store and buy something (ruining the only reason for stopping the pump on the exact dollar amount, to keep from waiting on change). Is this some kind of game of skill people like to play?

There are too many cars on the road for ignorant drivers to be out adding to the pure hell of everyday driving. Think back to when you almost failed the written part of the driving test, and figure out what you did not know. I cannot stand drivers who try to stop in the road when a traffic light is flashing yellow. A flashing yellow traffic light means slow down and proceed with caution, it does not mean *stop*. A flashing red light means stop and go like a stop sign. Also, when the traffic light is out due to power failure, you treat it like a four-way stop. Drivers need to learn how to let off the accelerator before you come to a stop. You will be amazed how much longer your vehicle will last if you quit abusing it. Do not accelerate all the way to a stop sign, slam on the brakes, and then start off like you are in a race. You are the people who complain when their brakes are worn out between every ten-to fifteen-thousand miles.

Road rage is pure stupidity. What is the point of getting mad while you are driving? In this day and age, you are going to get killed one day when you shoot that bird or honk your horn at the wrong idiot. You will just be another death statistic on our highways. Keep your gestures to yourself; keep your mouth shut, and lay off the horn. You need to learn how to be a defensive driver, not an offensive driver. You can usually tell the poor drivers on the road; they are the ones who drive around in beat-up cars that have not been repaired. This shows me they are not staying out of the way of other drivers.

Drivers need to learn how to drive all over again. I know that parking test you took to get your license really showed you how to drive, but you need to think about your driving skills and really think if you are doing it properly. I do not know who taught you how to drive, but people who change lanes rapidly over and over do not get anywhere, and any quicker than the rest of us Sunday drivers who stay in one lane and maintain a constant speed. Look around next time you are driving ten to twenty miles into town. The same jackasses you see jumping all over the road will get there about the same time as everyone else. There is a reason highways get clogged up at the entrance ramps and exit ramps. People will not take a gap or give a gap. This is one of the most basic driving skills. Jackasses think an extra twelve feet is going to make them late for work. There is no reason why you cannot let someone get onto the highway. You need to share the highway with everyone else on the road. Common courtesy is a thing of the past.

Drivers need to learn to give truckers the road and stay out of the way. Drivers need to understand that tractor-trailers weigh up to 80,000 pounds. You are flirting with death with a forty-ton monster that will kill you and not even know it. Truck drivers can hit you and run you off the road and never even feel it. Records have shown that truckers are a lot safer drivers than the average vehicle driver on the road. Truck drivers are at least given on the road testing, while regular drivers only have to show they can park a car and drive twenty feet.

Jackasses are everywhere when it comes to your health. Some people say they are as "healthy as an ox," yeah, they smell like one too! Everyone is an expert when it comes to fitness and general health. Someone has a scam waiting for you every time you read a magazine, watch television, or even read newspapers. Just think if you just try our new horny rabbit inbred goat root you will suddenly become a stallion in bed, your baldness will go away, and you will lose those love handles all within one week.

Exercise machine peddlers are jackasses. There are hundreds of companies peddling the newest exercise gadget on the market. These items mostly do not work, and the ones that do are not used by the people who purchase them. My Soloflex workout machine was one really expensive clothes hanging rack. Stop throwing your money away, and use what is around you to help you exercise. The best exercises in the world are found in the Charles Atlas books that show people how to exercise with household items. The hardest push-ups in the world are performed using three kitchen chairs. People need to exercise in any way, shape, or form that they can. People today have so many things going on in their lives that they cannot stop for thirty minutes to an hour for structured exercise. Do what you can. Take stairs instead of using elevators or escalators. Do a couple of push-ups while your hair is drying. Walk every chance you get. Do not try to structure an exercise plan if you have young children because children do not follow a schedule. The best exercise in the world is to take a child outside or to the park and chase them around for a while. You will get exhausted, and the child will still be pulling you to come on.

Weight loss plan pushers are jackasses. Everyone has the best weight loss plan, until you try it. Everyone has a better diet. Do not eat meat. Do not eat bread or pasta. Do not eat sugar. Who can follow a diet like these? I can assure you *no* diet will work if you have to cut out 100 percent of the things you love. I will let you in on the secret two ingredients you need to lose weight (just send $19.95 plus $29.95 shipping to…). If you look at every single weight loss drink, pill, fountain of youth, or whatever, they will all contain one or both of these: chromium and ginseng. Look at the ingredients, and you will see I am not blowing smoke. To lose weight you need to go to a Sam's Club, Wal-Mart, Target, or the like and buy a bottle of chromium picolinate. Chromium is what helps you lose weight and is a fraction of the cost if you buy it by itself. At Sam's Club, a bottle of chromium with 500 pills will cost you $8. Take two pills a day, and you will start to notice results within a month. This is the same diet ingredient as the expensive brands but without the fluffy ingredients to drive up the cost. Ginseng on the other hand will give you energy, which can relate to helping you lose weight (and a harder erection, if you are a man). Same plan with the ginseng, buy it by itself at Sam's Club or Wal-Mart. At Sam's Club, the bottle of ginseng is around $9. Good luck, lard ass.

Overweight people are jackasses. Going hand in hand with your weight loss is the fifty jelly doughnuts you jam down your throat on a daily basis. Your eating habits and weight is your responsibility. Do not try to blame anyone or anything. Aside from a very few health disorders, being overweight is due to too much intake of food and not enough exercise. You can start helping yourself by drinking diet sodas. If you cannot stand the taste of it, shut up and keep drinking it, you will get used to it. After you drink diet soda for a few weeks, you will not like the taste of regular sodas. Your taste buds will get off the sugar kick. Drinking diet soda will not fix your problems, but it is a start. You need to learn how to eat zero calorie foods. A zero calorie food is one that takes more calories to eat than it puts in your body. Celery, carrots, cabbage, and things like this are foods that help you lose weight. Salsa is one of the best foods. Stay away from fattening items like dressings, jams, jellies, mayonnaise, etc., that destroy all the good things the good foods are doing. Maybe I will write a full diet book later that people can actually follow. The main goal is to keep trying. If you fall off the wagon, dust yourself off, and get back on. Stick to a diet consisting of vegetables, meat in moderation, diet sodas, and no sweets, and you will lose weight. Throw in a little exercise, and you will be on your way.

Self-abusers are jackasses. I am one of the jackasses too. If you drink beer, liquor, wine, smoke cigarettes, do drugs, or do other harmful things to your body, you are a jackass. Alcohol will destroy your liver, kill your brain cells, get you punched in the face at a bar, make you beat your spouse, make you wreck your car, and probably will get you killed if you do it outside the home without a designated driver. Be careful. I do drink too much, but I always drink at home unless my designated wife is driving and not drinking. I have driven while intoxicated and was very lucky I did not get killed or arrested. I do not know about you, but driving using the one eye method to keep the lines from splitting is a hassle. I stopped getting behind the wheel after drinking over a decade ago and am really glad I did.

Cigarette smoking will kill you. Hopefully, only the idiots going after the tobacco companies are the only people dumb enough to not know this. How you could smoke and not know it will harm you is beyond me. You need to stop as soon as you can because the sooner you stop the sooner your body can try to repair the harm you have caused. How can you blame someone else for your stupidity? There are many new items on the market that will help. Hopefully, the insurance companies will start to help pay for these stop-smoking aids. The insurance companies are ignorant as to the costs I guess because they gladly pay for you to go to the doctor several times a year for bronchitis, but they will not pay for any aid to help you quit smoking. It seems they would try to save money. This new shot they have out now is supposed to be a miracle cure, but it costs $500. Most people cannot afford this at one time. Sure, it is cheaper in the long-run, but it is not affordable for most people at this time. Zyban helps, but your insurance will not cover it either, unless your doctor will write it up as Wellbutrin. Same drug, only Wellbutrin is written up for depression. Patches and gums help, but are the least helpful. From what I have experienced, the habit side of smoking (the use of hands, mouth, etc.,) is the hardest problem with quitting smoking. The main thing is to keep trying to quit because eventually you will. Either you will quit on your own, or you will quit when you die. Your choice.

Sex therapists and sex peddlers are jackasses. It will make you go blind. Why is a man who reads *Playboy* a pervert and a woman with a vibrator is just relieving tension? I do not understand the bias. Nudity and sex are getting more prevalent in the media, so be prepared to hide this from your children. Women are completely nude in everyday magazines, except for a little body paint. Entertainers seem to pose nude when their popularity goes down. Everyone tries to ban pornography, while the everyday media gets deeper into the nudity issue. I do not care if you want porno. If you like porno and nudity, that is fine; I think being a free American should allow you to look at this type of material if you choose (as long as minors are not involved). Why do some people get so bent out of shape over nudity? Get a damn life. Go complain about the violence in "Roadrunner" cartoons or something.

Sex is a great thing. Just try to have it regularly when you have young children. By the time you get everyone to bed, the house cleaned, and other work done, you are just too tired to care about sex. Single people say "Man, I could have sex every day," *That's bull;* they obviously have never been married. Sex becomes a chore over time, and the best thing you can do is to try and keep it interesting. Buy some sex toys so your children or in-laws will find them. Do it in different places and be willing to experiment. Nothing is better than having guests over for dinner, knowing you just had sex on the dinner table the night before. Nothing makes sex more exciting than when you are at the doctor having something removed from one of your orifices. Wear a wig; everyone would like to get some "strange" every once and a while.

Sex is great until you find out the hard way a child is on the way, and then it becomes the evil conception. Just a word to the wise, condoms do not fail. You do. If you put a condom on correctly, the chances of it failing are slim to none, unless the woman is not ready. If the woman was not ready, you failed as a man anyway and deserve to have a little reminder of your stupidity. If you cannot put on a condom and pinch the air out of the end, then you need to just keep beating off. Remember dumb people have dumb kids.

Homophobes are jackasses. Those who are afraid of homosexuals need to take a look at their own issues. All I hear is people saying they do not like television shows like *Will and Grace* or any other television show with homosexuals. Shut up, and get a life. If you cannot get past the homosexual part and enjoy a funny show, you are just immature. I do not care what people do with their lives, I am too busy living mine. The uproar over legalizing marriage in Massachusetts was ridiculous. Who cares? Homosexuals or lesbians getting married will not affect my wife, my children, me, or my life in any way. Find something better to do with your life than to cry about issues such as these.

Practicing Medicine

When I was in school, all the boys thought it would be "cool" to be a gynecologist because they would get to see nude women. Never did they think that the majority of the women in the world are *not* supermodels. Scary job. I have watched my wife give birth to both of our children, and I will tell you I have seen things fall out of my wife that I never thought I would see. I think every nurse in the hospital had their hands in my wife. Women have things falling or leaking out of them all the time. I have a newfound respect for gynecologists and proctologists.

Doctors are jackasses. Doctors have a license to steal. These people have one of the few professions out there where they can overcharge for their inability to fix your problem. I have been battling an ongoing problem with my esophagus and have been bounced around from doctor to doctor for tests. One doctor billed the insurance company over $200 to take my blood pressure, weight, and pulse rate. I was there for less than five minutes.

Doctors are known for screw-ups. You hear stories all the time about them leaving tools inside their patients. There is no real way of telling how many people have died because of doctor mistakes. I have heard of doctors operating on the wrong side of the body and amputating the wrong limb. I have heard cases of doctors removing hemorrhoids from patients who were there for other problems. Plastic surgeons are famous for crooked faces and lopsided breasts. The lists are endless, and the average American is the one who suffers at the hands of these butchers.

Malpractice insurance and medical lawsuits are a joke. Lovely people out there, who love to sue people, have screwed up our doctors to no end. Malpractice insurance rates have chased a lot of good doctors out of the field for fear of getting sued. Fraudulent cases are filed daily against doctors for mistakes or complications that could not have been prevented. Abuse of the malpractice insurance business has driven the costs of insurance and medical services through the roof. Doctors make mistakes all the time, but the majority of the malpractice cases I have read about are fraudulent. The lawsuits are ridiculous. Do you really deserve $10 million for pain and suffering for something that has not destroyed your life? You and fifteen generations of your family combined would never make this kind of money. Quit driving my insurance rates up!

Health insurance companies have a wonderful way of not paying claims. Hopefully, your state has a tough insurance commissioner to go after these morons to get them to pay your medical bills for you. I get bills all the time, and I do not know if they have or have not been paid. I get a bill that scares the hell out of me every time I go to the doctor, even though the insurance company eventually pays it. Insurance companies actually drive up the costs of medical care. The problem with my esophagus was diagnosed on my first visit to my general care doctor. I then had to go to other doctors and to the hospital six more times before they would do anything; each visit of course was charged to the insurance company as a separate visit. My problem was not a major one; I just could not eat food or drink water. No big ordeal.

Drug companies are really jackasses. Drugs cost too much! The actual costs of drugs are minimal. Drug companies have a great plan to figure out their drug costs. They spend 80 percent of the costs of drugs in marketing and advertising, 15 percent in research and testing, and about 5 percent for actual materials to make the drugs. The drug companies' marketing plans are so strong, people actually go to the doctors looking for certain drugs. People ask for drugs that have nothing to do with their problems because the people in the advertisements and commercials look so happy using that particular drug. It is amazing to see healthy people looking for antidepressants because the little cartoon figure in the commercial is *so* happy due to this drug.

Plastic surgeons and the people that use them are jackasses. Where is my hair? I will tell you where it is; it is growing down my neck to its final resting place on my back. Uh oh, it is time to get a new rug on my head. My left testicle hangs lower than the right one, I better get something done. My boobs are too small; my left boob is bigger, or I wear a size thirty-eight *long* bra, and it's sagging, so I better get something done. I have to wear a belt to hold my boobs up, I better get something done. Give me a break! People need to understand that no one is perfect, and even after these surgeries, they still will not be perfect. People, there is such a thing as boobs that are too big. I am just waiting for penis-enlargement surgery to become more mainstream, so I can hear about all the botched failures. There will be thousands of lawsuits due to crooked penises everywhere. Penises that will not get erect will be the norm. I would love to have a very large, limp penis to show my wife. Great to look at, but it does not work worth a damn!

Alternative medical providers are jackasses. Do your research because a lot of herbs actually work quite well, but some herbs can kill you or make your heart beat irregularly and cause a great deal of other problems. Every fad herb that has come out over the past decade has had problems, with the exception of a few. Most large stores now sell herbs, so that you do not have to pay through the nose to go to some old lady selling dried rhino horn in her lair. Specialist herb shops are good for whole herbs such as flower petals to make tea and things of that nature, but do not go to an herbal store to buy pills. You are just wasting your money. Acupuncturists and aroma therapists have ways of helping some situations, but not all. Chiropractors have been known to do more harm than good in a lot of cases. I personally know a man who has been going to a chiropractor for over ten years and still has to go twice a month, or he cannot function. Insurance does not pay for this. I made the mistake of cracking my wife's back one time, and now I have to do this all the time. Something about getting your back cracked makes you need it all the time. I will just suffer periodically through my own back pain, to keep from getting addicted to a chiropractor and going broke.

The Anal Probe

Political correctness is ruining America as we know it. Anal people who have no lives worry constantly about what people are saying and doing. Some people get offended by everything that is said or done by everyone. You cannot leave the house or open your mouth without someone getting offended. People can be anal in many ways, and I will discuss a few below.

Excessively clean and organized people are jackasses. You can only get something clean to the extent of wasting your time. My poor wife had to go to a doctor as a child because her mother bathed her so much, her skin was damaged. The doctor told her mother to stop bathing her several times a day. She was cleaning her skin off. Some people are excessively organized. This is not a problem when you are single, but when you get married and have children, you will go mad due to the disarray that soon follows. If you know someone like this, you need to really fire them up; go to their home and lay a towel down on the counter, or take off your hat and throw it on the sofa. This will drive them up a wall. You will be sent immediately to hell by them or at least in their minds. They may even get the anti-organized voodoo dolls out to punish you.

People who push stupid issues are jackasses. Get a life! I understand people having strong feelings on some issues, but come on people! People actually love to push foolish issues (that the average American could care less about) to the point of violence. Peace lovers are the most violent people I have ever heard of.

Flag fighters are jackasses. The flag issues of late are one of the most anal issues ever in history. The most outspoken anal people usually win these cases. The average American is not going to stop their lives to go argue about a state flag. These flag fighters say to hell with history. We all need to attack anything that we disagree with, so that every government painting, picture, and government symbol will all be changed to big giant smiley faces. Every state must have a big smiley face on their flag. Nude paintings and sculptures must have smiley faces over any offending parts. *Go home!* People will never agree with everything all the time on any issue. Why do we have to shut down the state to deal with this kind of whining? You do not like the state flag, and I do not like your appearance. So what? We as Americans do not need to cater to every whining bunch that does not like something.

Peace lovers and war protesters are jackasses. Sometimes war or a fight is necessary to accomplish a goal or protect your country. I am proud that someone in America has the gonads to stand up for us. Too many times our country has catered to the evil and the haters of America. This is a sign of weakness. Our media says that our country is divided when it comes to the war issue, and this gives them more reason to attack us. You may not agree with the war in the Middle East, but you are not going to change it. You should show your support for your country by shutting the hell up! You need to understand that the average American does not and will not ever know all the facts that led us into war with Afghanistan and Iraq. You did not know the facts before, during, or after any conflict the United States has ever been in, and that is the way it should be. I want my country to take care of business for me, so that I can enjoy my life as a free American. Peace lovers preach peace, peace, peace, while the terrorists are next to them lighting fuses. The media has already told you too much.

The Ten Commandments haters are jackasses. Do we need to rewrite the Bible and all of history to keep from offending you? With a daily barrage of thousands of advertisements, signs, stupid drivers, stupid co-workers, stupid bosses, stupid children, or whatever, how can you get upset about a list of beliefs the majority of the world believes in? What is there to disagree about with the commandments? Do you think it is OK to murder? If you do not believe in the religion that came up with this list, fine, but do not deny others the right to see the Ten Commandments. In America, we should not make it a habit to hide anything to do with someone's religion. I understand the separation of church and state, but I also believe you should not stomp on other people's rights because you are offended. Do I go around snatching the rug out from under a Muslim's knees while they are praying? *No!* Then stay away from my Ten Commandments! I do not know of anyone, from any religion, that does not believe in the Ten Commandments. The God mentioned in the Ten Commandments could be your God, unless you are an atheist. Unless you are a bigamist, everything else should make sense to you.

People who are offended by everything are jackasses. PC police to the rescue. Does every newspaper, magazine, and television show need to censor every single word spoken or written for offensive phrases or even gestures? You have the right as a free American to turn the channel on the TV and radio, or change papers or magazines any time you feel that someone has offended you. A free country means that offenders can say any stupid thing they want, but they have to be aware of the consequences, such as lost viewership, listeners, or readers. As a result of stupid behavior, the next thing the offenders will lose is advertising revenue and possibly their jobs. That is how a free society works. You are free to be stupid, and sometimes there is an undesired outcome as a result of your stupidity.

I cannot believe people are offended by breast-feeding. Breast-feeding is the single most important thing a mother can do for the health of her baby, and people are offended by it. If you are offended by someone breast-feeding, you must have been a bottle-fed baby because you obviously missed something important when you were born. Maybe you received some cow ignorance or something. Cry, cry, cry.

As you can see, America is being conquered by ignorant, anal people who like to push their beliefs on the majority. Only in America can a simpleminded minority rule by stupidity and ignorance.

English: The "Mutt" of All Languages

Our education system is full of jackasses. Education is the core of our society. We need *one* language in this country: *English*. If you cannot speak it, *learn it!* If you want to be an American and live in America, then you need to learn English. If I go live in Russia, I would have to learn Russian; the Russians would not all learn English to keep from offending me. English is one of the most difficult languages to learn, but somehow, we have accomplished learning it for hundreds of years. I know the PC police have reached *Webster's Dictionary* and are getting them to add words that are not a part of the English language. You may think you have accomplished something by getting slang terms admitted to the dictionary, but you have not. Go to a job interview speaking slang terms, and do not be upset when you leave the interview jobless. Do not come crying to me, because *I do not care!*

School counselors are jackasses. Did you realize that when you were in high school, no one told you which jobs were the best? They all say the same things about doctors and lawyers, but everyone cannot be doctors and lawyers. You never get the truth when you ask about a certain field. This is the reason why you have so many college graduates working in bars and restaurants.

From what I have seen, the best college fields in today's market are computer-related, medicine, secondary teaching, management, and sales related to financial markets. Please do your research before you pick a major. Look in the papers for what jobs are in demand. Look at U.S. labor statistics. Find people in the fields you are considering and ask them how it has been for them. Do not rely on someone to tell you which field to go into if they have not done it themselves, they are ignorant about the issue anyway.

School recruiters are jackasses. Recruiters have one goal when it comes to you, to get you to go to their school for the money. They do not care that you might have talent in a certain field; if they did, you would be receiving a scholarship. There are good schools and bad schools at the college level. You need to find someone who went to that school and discuss it with them before you make any decisions. All the advertisements, the brochures, and fluff you get from a certain school are just to sweeten the appearance, to get you into their doors. Unlike high school, with college, the money follows the students, and the students actually have a choice where their money is going to go. Most students cannot afford to go to private colleges, so you have to do your homework. You need to try and find out how many graduates of whichever school actually found employment after graduation. Talk to as many people you can that went to that particular school.

School administrators are complete jackasses. The system has failed our children. There is no discipline in school any longer. No more paddling, no detention, no suspension when needed, and definitely no expulsion (unless it is for something stupid, like having a butter knife in your car when you are moving to another home). Punishment in school is being phased out by jackass parents who do not want their little babies to be responsible for their stupid actions. This is because the stupid things children do sometimes reflect the stupid parenting they have received. Parents are failures and it shows with our children.

When did oral sex in classrooms begin? How could this possibly happen? Every class I was ever in had a teacher's pet that would tattle at the slightest sign of disobedience. Where was the teacher? Why did the other students allow this to happen? The parents of these children are complete failures, along with every other parent of every student in that school. The parents of the blow-happy students now do not want their children to be punished. Schools have gone to hell, and all we can do is watch.

The correct answers are not needed in school now. I have news for you; effort only counts while having sex. Sex is the only thing you can do wrong, and it is still so right! The rest of the time, there is a right and wrong answer. Essay questions have some leeway. We are teaching our children that it is OK to get it wrong, as long as you tried. Close should not count in education. Right is right; wrong is wrong. Why do you think so many people hate doing math? Do you want your employers to give a good attempt at getting your paycheck right; do you just want them to try? What about the bank? Do you want them to add your bank transactions using school methods? Stop trying to keep from hurting the student's feelings. We have all been upset about being wrong. Everyone will get wrong answers. Let them grow up, as we all have in the past, from experience!

Pay the teachers a decent salary. Our teachers are giving away grades. Quit wasting money in other areas, and pay these teachers a decent wage. They have hard jobs. They take work home. If you expect our children to learn, you do not want an angry, underpaid teacher trying to do it. All they will do is try to stick your kid on

Ritalin to shut him or her up. It is amazing how fast teachers try to put children on these drugs. They do not tell the parents such things as once they have taken these drugs they can never join the Armed Forces. That would be honest. The drug manufacturers are hurting though. They have spent the billions of dollars they have made selling Ritalin to our children, on yachts, mansions, and jewelry, I guess they can because now, they are aiming this drug at adults. How did adults survive before these drugs came along? Maybe Beaver, June, Ward, and Wally were all hooked.

We need to secure our schools. Do not let children leave school unless they have parental consent, and the parents know where the child is going. Give the schools more security to keep out unwanted children, drug dealers, anal parents, and people of that nature. Whatever happened to hall monitors? Sure they were nerds, but they could help notify authorities if a problem turned up.

School vouchers will correct a lot of problems within our school system because word of mouth travels fast in our society. Word will get out about all the stupid abuses in a certain school, and the parents can decide to move their children wherever they think they will get the best education. The only problem is there are not enough private schools to handle the massive move out of the government schools.

Racial warlords in education are jackasses. The new conspiracy in schools is the debate over black scores vs. white scores on testing. Some people call this a culture issue. It is really a failure of two groups: the parents, who did not require their children to learn in school, and the student, for picking the wrong friends. It is, and will always be easier to hang out with friends on the playground or wherever. Why did your child not pick kids to hang out with in the library? Oh! Because that is not *cool!* Well, you just teach your child it is OK to be "cool" and stupid, see how far they get on that. We also hear people preaching about the rich versus poor kids' scores in school. This argument makes a little more sense than the race issue because rich parents do not rear their children anyway; they have nannies or tutors to teach their children and keep them out of their hair.

Ebonics is for jackasses. To anyone who agrees with Ebonics, you are a jackass and ignorant. You are further dividing classes of people and ruining any chance your child has of leading a productive life. Just look at how the south is viewed by people in most of America. Southerners use a lot of slang terms like: *ya'll* and *come back now, ya' hear.* Everything is a contraction in the southern slang. People view the Cajuns in the same way. Americans view both as inferior, and now you want to further the black cause by teaching Ebonics. How intelligent! There will always be dialects depending on where you live, but do not separate a race with a language. Northerners have never eaten grits, but they eat hominy, which is the same damn thing, only larger. How do you drive a "cah" anyway? I do not want to go to a "bah" with you for a drink. Everyone thinks everyone else is stupid anyway, so do not make it worse. These divisions exist and will always exist. Any country the size of America will always have different slangs and dialects, but we all need to base them on the English language. We all may pronounce words differently, and some may put several words together to make one, but at least we understand each other. We need to learn the English language as it is spoken in America, not in England; we need to speak English like it is spoken on the news, *Mr. Roger's Neighborhood, Sesame Street,* and other educational television shows. I do not know about you, but I do not want my children learning English by listening to the *Beverly Hillbillies*, the late Cajun cook Justin Wilson, the BBC in England, or some hip-hop rap group. I want my children to learn the traditional American way, somewhere in the middle of all of them.

Hyphenated Americanism

Anyone hyphenating his or her nationality is a jackass. I want to provide just a few definitions of nationality for those who insist on putting hyphens in the descriptions of themselves. Your race is what your ethnic background is. Your nationality is the country you were born in. A Caucasian man born in Africa is an African. A black man born in Vietnam is Vietnamese. If you are born in America to parents who live in America, then you are an American. Africa has nothing to do with it. I have never met a black person who wanted to go live in Africa, nor do I want to go live in England or Europe. Be proud of your heritage if you want, but do not let it get in the way of your advancement in the country you are supposed to be loyal to. Do not let people convince you to further delay the integration of black people by playing these games. You are making life worse for yourself and for your children. By pursuing these racial divisions, you will keep the white people from allowing you to coexist as one group—as "Americans."

I am no racist, nor am I a bigot (I hate *everyone*). When I first moved out of my parents' home, I lived with a black man and a white woman (all of us were single). Race was never an issue! We were too busy trying to live our lives. We never discussed race. We had a lot more important things to worry about: paying rent, getting better jobs, girls, dating, what's for dinner, and a thousand other things. I think slavery was brutally wrong, whether you were a black slave or a white slave (that is right, white slaves; read on).

Race-card players are jackasses. Everyone wants to play the race card in any argument. I have had employees who did not show up to work for several days at a time without calling. The day they got fired, they said it was because they were black. I said, "*No*, it is because you are sorry!" Whether you are black, white, Mexican, Vietnamese, Spanish, Latino, Italian, or whatever, *if you are sorry, I have no need for you!* Too many times people try to blame their problems on their race instead of their work or personal ethics. People have sorry parents all the time and perform well as adults. People grow up poor and become good citizens. People come out of gang-ridden neighborhoods and stay sober and out of trouble with the law. Why are you so different? You will reap what you sow. Look at all the great black men and women who have succeeded through hard times in America; what did they do differently from you? Most successful blacks in America did not get that way through racial quotas and affirmative action.

Racists and bigots are jackasses. Racism exists and will always exist, but it goes *both* ways. Blacks show hatred toward whites also. We have to work together as a group to see that racism does not tear America apart. As it is now, whites hate blacks, blacks hate whites, Latinos hate whites and blacks, and blacks and whites hate Latinos. If you throw a few Italians, Vietnamese, Laotians, Greeks, and all the others together with all the other race-haters, we have ourselves a great mess. This problem is usually never the child's fault. Ignorant racist parents breed ignorant racist children, white, black, or whatever you want to call yourself this week. As they say, "Why can't we all just get along?"

The original enslavers were jackasses. England and America did not start slavery. As a matter of fact, for hundreds of years, the first slaves were white. Nobody will tell you that though. Most Americans, white and black alike, think slavery started with America. This is *not* how slavery started, and it was near the end of the slave trade. Most people think slavery was a bunch of white people going to Africa to kidnap people as slaves. This is not true either. People need to understand that slavery has been around since the first recorded languages. There are recordings in ancient Sumer of slaves that were white, all white. These slaves dated back before 2300 BC, and these slaves were treated as possessions and had to go with their owners to the afterlife. There are burial grounds with people buried with seventy slaves. This was brutal. Ancient Greece, Mesopotamia, Egypt, and Rome could not have survived their way of life without the cheap labor of slaves. Some people were brought up as slaves from the time of birth. A Serb was the name of a class of people that would become slaves. Most slaves were acquired by war. Instead of making people prisoners after a war, the conquering leader would make them into slaves. White slaves were used all throughout time, up until the movement into the Americas. The slave trade from Africa did not start until the 1400s and 1500s. Portugal and Spain were the two major importers of slaves from Africa. Portugal and Spain possessed territories in Africa, where they could get slaves from.

The major slave trade from Africa started when the tribal chiefs, up and down the coast of Africa, started to collect their own tribesmen to sell as slaves. Slaves from Africa were sold like sugar (a commodity). The first slaves started showing up in America in the 1600s, both black and white. Due to the territorial expansion in America, Europeans imported more slaves through the 1700s. Importation of slaves stopped mostly by 1808, when President Thomas Jefferson abolished the foreign trade of slaves. Between 1790 and 1800, the census stated that the black population was around 700,000 to 900,000 people, out of a total of 4 million people in America. By the time the civil war ended, the black population was up to almost four million. This massive expansion of the black population did not come from more slave imports, but from new children being born to slaves. The slaves in America had a much better way of life than people in Africa, and the infant death rate was radically better in America, and it still is today.

Less than 5 percent of all slaves came to America. Most slaves from Africa went to Central America and Brazil. Slavery was cruel and harsh, but the slaves did survive. People also do not know that black people also owned slaves. When slavery was abolished after the Civil War, the people you believe wanted to free the slaves also wanted to send the slaves back to Africa, as they were doing in other countries. Read the histories of Sierra Leone and Liberia to learn how other slaves were sent back to Africa. People need to tell you the facts, but they will not; you have to go out and learn the truth for yourself.

People hiding the truth from blacks are jackasses. The black people in America do not understand the complete picture. Depending on who is counting, the U.S. census reports that Spanish-speaking people actually outnumber blacks in this country. Black people account for only 12 to 15 percent of the U.S. population. Most blacks do not know this, from my experience. The black population, by number, is concentrated in five areas. The largest numbers, by city, are New York, Chicago, Detroit, Philadelphia, and Los Angeles. By percentage of population per state, it is Washington DC, Mississippi, Louisiana, South Carolina, and Georgia. By black population per state, it is New York, California, Texas, Florida, and Georgia. These numbers may not mean a hill of beans to you, but it should. Because the black population is less than 15 percent of the total U.S. population, equality is a long way away. The state/area with the highest percentage of blacks is Washington DC, at 60 percent. The next closest state is Mississippi at 36 percent, then Louisiana at 32 percent, and then South Carolina at 29 percent. For the remainder of the states, the number drops to the 5 to 10 percent range rather quickly. As you can see, just by numbers alone, the black population still has a small voice at this time in national politics and voting. Blacks do have a strong voice in the states and cities mentioned earlier. As the black population spreads out across our nation, instead of concentrating in certain major areas, you will see more attention brought to your causes. You have to also understand that the women in our country outnumber men and have yet to feel equal in politics, earning power, and in the workforce. Only more time will correct these problems.

Most racial leaders are jackasses. We have some wonderful leaders on the ignorance bandwagon. They do not care about blacks in general. You have your Jesse's, your Al's, and a lot of others who love to use Reverend in their titles. Usually not very righteous in their own lives; these men will not share the facts with their so-called brothers. Jesse had an out-of-wedlock child after an adulterous affair, bought his fling a $300,000 home, and gave her a $120,000-a-year allowance. Who actually pays for this adulterous affair? His followers, who keep giving him money, do. Keeping the general black population in the dark about the facts of any issue is their strongest suit. Every story has facts, and these leaders spin the facts around to fit their own agendas. Do you want to know what their agendas are?

Self-promotion and self-enrichment are the name of the game. They are always coming to the rescue by turning a non-racial issue into some kind of race war. "Let us keep hate alive," is what they need to be saying, because that is what they are doing!

Hey! Watch This

Our wonderful media (e.g., newspapers, magazines, television, and radio)! Our media in America is run and managed by the higher upper-class people, who grew up with silver spoons in their mouths and nannies to wipe their butts. These people do not understand the plights of the average American. They do not have to deal with the same issues that the rest of us have to deal with. This is probably why all the media people are liberals and Democrats. Why do entertainers always threaten to leave the country if so-and-so wins but never leave? Get out! You do not belong in this country.

Magazine, television, newspaper, and radio editors and programmers are jackasses. While America is preparing for and fighting wars, our rocket scientists in the media love to disclose the movement, locations, firepower, and numerous other intelligence items to everyone. One magazine I read leading up to the war in Iraq had actual maps showing the locations of all the U.S. battleships, troops, bases, warheads, and even more that I cannot remember. Our enemies can read too, dumb-asses! I want my country to go over there, and take care of business. We already know too much as it is. Ever heard of covert operations?

Biased media personnel are jackasses. The absolute strongest power of the media is the use of *omission!* Every story, quote, phrase, and description ever printed or spoken, can be completely changed by leaving out a word or two or taking the words out of context. You should be quoted exactly as you have spoken, with all of the related words, to give the correct context of a story. How many police beatings have you seen where the media will not show you the crook beating the hell out of a policeman? None! You will only see the police beating the law-breaker to death after they have acted like a complete fool. Every story we hear has a slant on it. Usually everything is spun in the liberal Democrat view. No one hears the whole truth about anything anymore. You literally have to read several newspapers and magazines on one subject just to get to the real truth. Everyone loves to say they do fair reporting, but unless you own your own print media or TV/radio station, you are going to be biased. I have heard stories that even in the food section of newspapers, the reporters like to throw in attacks coming from the left toward Republicans, if you can believe that. There is a reason the Fox News Channel is so successful. They actually cover the story and not the slant. The newspaper editorial pages are another story; their reporting is so slanted to the left that the print on the pages actually looks slanted. Do your research before you believe anything you read in the paper or magazine, or hear on the radio or TV. The norm used to be the facts, now the facts are twisted by who is telling the story.

Poor reporters and editors are jackasses. Errors in reporting are running rampant. People tell stories or print them before the facts are in. Witnesses gathered by the news tell incorrect statements. Have you ever noticed that in any event, the reporters seem to find the dumbest person in a crowd of one hundred to tell what they saw? Find "Boo Got Shot" on the Internet, and you will understand a perfect example of this. The story could be on foreign affairs, and the reporter will grab a tobacco-spitting, cousin-marrying, gun-shooting hillbilly to tell the story (no offense meant to the hillbilly, just the reporter).

Negative reporters are jackasses. We are in a war, idiot. I do not need to wake up every single day of this war with, "another GI is dead." I know people are going to die. That is what happens when people are shooting guns at each other. No one ever reports all the good we have done in Afghanistan and Iraq. We do not hear that the Iraqi people have more power to more locations than they have ever had before. The media will only tell you about the deaths, the destruction, and the other idiot reporters who like to chase wars.

Non-news reporters are jackasses. I do not care if someone's cat is trapped down a well somewhere. I do not care if the town where the cat was shut down to save the damn cat, while houses burned down and people were getting robbed, and all the while, every policeman, fireman, and ambulance was at your well. Go find a news story, and quit filling time with stories of the dumb!

Actors are jackasses. Move to another country if you want to. Your job is to entertain with your acting skills. When you go home, no one cares what you think. Not all, but most actors should refrain from speaking any time they are off the set/stage. Every time we hear from actors, it seems that they make fair-minded people think the actor is an idiot. Every day in the news, we hear of some idiotic statement from someone in Hollywood. Most actors are usually slanted far left or far right. The fair-minded actors seem to stay out of the public spotlight, probably because they are intelligent enough to keep their mouths shut when they have nothing to say.

Athletes are jackasses. I have no problem with someone making millions of dollars a year bringing fans into the stadiums. The problem occurs when you have one athlete making so much money that they break the team's budget. One player will make more than half the team combined. The result of this is the money gets passed back to the consumer (me). If I am not mistaken, most average Americans cannot afford to go to baseball, football, or basketball games anymore. I have received free tickets to baseball games and found out the hard way how much the extras cost. With a family of four going to a game, paying for tickets, parking, a few hot dogs, and maybe a beer or twelve, you have to spend over $200 for one game. The costs of going to a sports game are far outpacing the increase in people's incomes. I foresee a major drop in attendance over the next few years that will change the way people look at these costs. You have to remember the fans are the ones paying the paychecks of these talented players. Sooner or later, the fans will say, "Enough."

Sports-fan groupies are jackasses. "Arnold groped my butt over twenty years ago. I know I did nothing then, but now he is running for governor." Please. Why did you stay quiet for this long? If what he did back then was so bad, you would have sued him. I guess everybody needs his or her fifteen seconds of fame and publicity. You always hear, "I was afraid" as the answer to why they did not report it. Why now? Next thing you know, someone will come up with a semen-soaked dress they wore after one of his competitions. Kobe had to rape a girl who came to his room? Whatever! Mike raped? Maybe. People seem to play complete ignorance when it comes to sports figures. People do not understand that athletes have groupies like rock stars and could, if they choose, have any girl at any time while on the road or at home. Women flock to male athletes like flies to shi*. Panties are thrown at them. Phone numbers. Women would cheat on their husbands in a second to have sex with a sports hero. Other than Wilt Chamberlain, players don't usually talk about how many times they have had sex with groupies.

Musicians are jackasses. I listen to all types of music: classical, rock, pop, country, blues, and even rap. Some musicians have great talent in their fields, but they need to learn when to shut the hell up too. Just dance, play, or sing, and do not say anything outside the studio or concert. Poor role models are everywhere. People need to listen to the music and not the words to today's songs. It seems as if the music keeps getting better, while the lyrics have all gone to hell. This is a free country and we do allow them to do this. Musicians find out the hard way when they go too far. Fans disappear. Is country music the only wholesome music left? Where is Toby?

Television talk show hosts are jackasses. Everyone thinks TV talk-show hosts are gospel. Leave it to Jerry to show us the real Americans out there. Ms. W seems to have everybody hooked on ignorance and feelings. These shows prey on the stupid, like a lottery taxes the stupid; these people draw them like flies. I know of people who cannot leave their home while a daytime talk show is on. Get a damn VCR, or get a life.

Censors are jackasses. So-called artists should be able to write, sing, or play anything they want, if they can find people stupid enough to listen to them. If they can coordinate that many dumb people into a following, then more power to them. Everything from music, television, radio, and even the cartoons are being stomped on by censors. Let the public decide what they want and do not want. This is a perfect example of too much power being given to the stupid.

Radio talk-show hosts are *not* jackasses. They are all conservative and have the gonads to say what needs to be said. Sometimes they offend, but most of the time, they hit the nail on the head. People who dislike radio talk-show hosts have never listened to them for more than one day. I thought all talk shows were stupid, until I actually started listening regularly to Neal Boortz from WSB Radio in Atlanta. That was the day I saw the light, you might say.

Mr. Boortz taught me to go out and get the truth, to not believe anything I read or hear unless I know it is the truth. I have been his listener for many years now. I do not agree with everything he says, but most of his ramblings make sense. Along with his anti-Boortz cohort Royal Marshall and his environmentalist Belinda Skelton, they put on a hilarious show that presents all different views on all subjects. Every day is riddled with the all-too-familiar stupidity of the day. I think he vacations about ten weeks out of the year with all the millions he is making now, as opposed to his earlier years, working seven jobs while going to law school. Working 160 hours a week and sleeping 8, he has finally made himself a success.

Mr. Boortz turned me on to Sean Hannity and Bill O'Reilly, both who are on the Fox News channel and have radio talk shows of their own. These two men are not afraid to approach issues that the mainstream media will not touch. Both men seem to show an honest and direct approach to getting the facts. Blunt and to the point is the way I like my news, without all the fluff. If you have not listened to Neal Boortz, Sean Hannity, and Bill O'Reilly, you need to give them a try. You will be glad you did. You need to stop listening to that pop, country, rap, or whatever, and give talk radio the chance to educate you and convert you from ignorance.

The Environ "Mental" ists

With all the advances we have made as a society, why can the scientists not figure out ways to clean our air, eliminate pollutants, make efficient electricity, and clean our water?

Environmental researchers are jackasses. Am I the only person in America that thinks we should be able to figure out what to mix with carbon dioxide to make it more favorable to our planet? You add hydrogen and oxygen to get water. We can take gold from a liquid solution with electricity to gold plate car emblems; what can we add to carbon dioxide to make it safe?

I think solar power is the key to our future. It is free, will never end, and is there for most of the day. Wind power is a joke, water does not supply 10 percent of anyone's needs, and nuclear is very dangerous to terrorist attack. The average American does not know that we still get most of our power in most areas of America from burning coal and natural gases. If we would transfer any of the millions being spent on idiotic things to solar energy research, we would be able to make solar power more efficiently and affordably. There is no reason solar power is only 15 to 30 percent efficient with all of our advances in technology. The average home can run completely off of solar power stored in batteries, and the homeowner can actually sell the additional power back to the power companies, but for some reason a decent system costs over $15,000 to install on the average-sized home. Who could afford this? Solar panels on your roof may not be as pretty as stained, rotten shingles, but

I think people would get over it as soon as they stopped paying $200 a month in power bills. Why is this happening? Just think, if California were able to get solar power running efficiently, they would not have to have rolling blackouts and energy rates that are higher than every other state in the country. For some strange reason, they keep chasing wind energy. Where I live, the sun shines a lot steadier and longer than the wind blows. I guess this only makes sense to me because nothing is being done.

The oil companies are jackasses. Oil companies are still running the world. This is the biggest reason we have not found alternative fuel sources. The big oil companies do not want anyone devising a plan to take any money out of their pockets. Someone needs to put a leash on these companies so that America can get ready for the future. We are eventually going to have problems with oil and natural gas resources, because no one knows how much there actually is. I understand we have millions of barrels of oil stored somewhere in America for just such a problem, but it is not the answer for the long term. This oil problem will not happen in my lifetime, but we need to find the answers *now*. At the rate we are going, by the time the crisis arises, it will be too late to start looking for answers. Environmentalists are getting in the way of correcting one major problem: acquiring our own oil. "Save the forests" is all we ever hear. We have vast amounts of oil sitting beneath Alaska, and we cannot touch it because of the environmentalists. Has anyone seen how big Alaska is compared to the rest of the United States? If we pumped in Alaska we could start to relieve our dependency on foreign oil.

Water polluters are jackasses. We are starting to see signs of water shortages all over America. We cannot water our grass except on certain days. The price of water keeps going up and the supply cannot go up unless we do something about it. One thing to remember is matter cannot be created or destroyed. All we ever hear about is water resources drying up; where is the water going? Water cannot disappear; it has to go somewhere, either downstream, underground, or in the air. People keep crying about the ice caps melting due to global warming. So what! When ice caps melt, they release water, which adds more water to the oceans, which adds more water to the air to be dropped as rain elsewhere. Water has a great way of filtering itself. I call it nature's great distillery. Water evaporates leaving behind any contamination or minerals, then drops down to earth as fresh water. Unfortunately, the fresh rain drags down our industrial pollutants out of the air with it. There should be other ways to purify water that can benefit the procedures we have now. We still are unable to take ocean water and efficiently make it drinkable. Why? Can we not pump water up from the ocean into a deserted valley, dam it off, and let the water soak into the water table beneath the ground as fresh water, after being filtered by the soil? Just an idea; you work on it some more.

The Law of the Land: Well, It Used to Be

The average American's Bill of Rights:

1. You have the right to pray to any God if you believe in one. The government will not get in the way unless some anal people get involved. You can say or print any stupid, idiotic thing you want, but beware, someone may beat the crap out of you or sue you for doing so. The press can say or print all the incorrect, left-wing, and liberal untruths they want and to spin the truth to fit their agendas. You and all your drunken friends can gather together peacefully and make complete fools of yourselves. You may piss and moan to the government any time you want something free that other taxpayers paid for; this includes the big-screen television you bought while you were on welfare.

2. You have the right to shoot yourself with the gun you purchased illegally at the monster truck show. You can blame someone else when you do something stupid, like letting your child get shot with the gun you did not protect them from. You can go out and kill animals to make yourself feel manly. You can wear all the camouflage outfits you want. You can have your child wear camouflage underwear if you so desire. You can shoot beer cans off fence posts to make yourself feel like Dirty Harry. You can

play "cops and robbers" with your buddies as long as no one gets killed.

3. While not at war, you will not have to let one of our underpaid soldiers into your rat-and roach-infested home, to sleep on your doggie-toilet carpet and child-vomit-covered furniture, not that they would want to anyway.

4. You can rest assured that no one wants to search your porn collection. Your home (which you cannot find your children in) will be left alone, unless you say something stupid and allow it. Your car will not be searched, unless you forget to put out your joint or that white powder still hanging out of your nose. Your body, which has not been bathed in days, will not be searched. No one will take your stuff, unless you break one of the 150,000 laws on the books in America. For the government to violate these rights, all they have to do is have probable cause; which means if you eat the last donut at the donut shop, you are likely to go to jail later that day.

5. You can take this right to court with you as a "get out of jail free card" if you are in trouble with someone else. You do not have to admit that you broke one of the numerous laws that no one knows about anyway. When your partner in crime gets caught, you can use this right to send him up the river without telling on yourself. This right says that a group of morons like yourself will have to fry you in serious crimes, unless you can get them to think you are the tooth fairy, Santa Claus, or the devil; in that case you get to go to happy land and take drugs all day. You can only be tried one time for each stupid thing that you do. You can only be electrocuted for killing your wife one time. No one

will kill you, steal your precious lava lamps, tie you up in chains, or hide you in a closet without following the law. No one will take your stuff, unless they say they need it or the local shopping center will pay your officials more tax money; in this case, you will receive pennies on the dollar for your stuff. This right is shot to hell if you are in the military; in that case you are just screwed.

6. You have the right to a speedy trial. Speedy means two months for a traffic ticket, one year for molesting one of your dogs or pigs, and two years for using your second right to shoot someone. You have the right to be publicly humiliated due to your idiotic actions and to have your bad name hit the media faster than steam starts coming off of cow manure. You will be judged by another group of cow-tipping friends or neighbors in the state and area where your trailer is parked (wheels on or off). You have the right to know why you are behind bars, as if you did not know already that you did the crime; which is possible due to the number of laws we have; no one could know whether they were breaking one anyway. You will get to see people that tell a better lie than you do, as they make you look like a fool, whether you are guilty or not, which you probably are. You can get all your drunk, toothless friends to come to the trial with you and lie about what an upstanding citizen you are. You can use taxpayer money to provide a lawyer for you who does not care whether you fry or not, because he will be twenty cases past yours when you meet your first prison boyfriend.

7. In a crime valued at over $20, you have the right to be judged by the same group of drunk, wife-beating, powder-snorting,

upstanding citizens who live near you, as mentioned in your earlier rights. Once this group of anal, politically correct, racially motivated, uneducated people have decided whether you can continue to freely be dumb, no other court can put you through this embarrassment again; unless they want to alter the law or use a loophole to do it again.

8. Since you are broke, this right is pointless but states that you will only have to hock your trailer to get your bail money to get out of jail. They can only squeeze so much blood out of a rock, so they cannot fine you more than the cost of a carton of cigarettes, unless it is a serious crime like putting up yard-sale signs. Your punishment has to be fair according to the way the judge or jury feels that day; if the judge has a case of green-apple splatters, you are going to the chair for stealing that beef jerky and six-pack. No one will make you do any cruel punishment other than going to sit in jail and eat, sleep, and live a better life than the average poor person does in America.

9. You have rights that no one knows yet, which apply to crimes you do not know you committed yet, because your politicians have not changed them sixty-seven times yet, because the U.S. Constitution was written by men who had not lost their minds yet.

10. If a right is not given to you in the Constitution, it does not mean one cannot be made up really fast by the states or other people to screw you over in a hurry. Others have the rights to play with the words and meanings of the Constitution in anyway they see fit. Every right can be slanted, spun, or turned into a racial attack or a civil rights violation in any trial, suit, or news

story, as long as someone makes money or gains publicity by doing so. Above and before all else, your right to be an ignorant, foolish, and selfish individual will be upheld if you can say one of your other rights has been violated.

In conclusion, you have to get mad in America to get anything done, because jackasses make the majority of laws and decisions. The average American is too busy leading their lives to bother with such foolishness, but you will have to become one of these jackasses also, or nothing will ever change for the better. People who have nothing but enrichment, notoriety, and selfishness as their agendas are sucking America down a hole. We have to get out there and change the things we disagree with, and it seems the only way to do so is to become what we hate.

All of America wants to know how you feel and what really upsets you. Please feel free to send us any notes, scribbles, essays, or whatever form of expression you would like at:

Angry Americans

PO Box 160

Haralson, GA 30229

We may use it in one of our upcoming books about Americans. You will have nothing to gain except getting your voice heard. We will make sure the president, vice president, and the U.S. Congress all have a chance to read how you feel.

By writing to us, you give us permission to use your words in one of our upcoming books. You will be given credit for what you have written. Please include your name, city, and state, so that we can find out what part of America is the angriest.

Please do yourself a favor and go out and find the *truth* about everything; do not trust anyone to teach you the facts. Someone always has a hidden agenda, even when they say they are being honest. Unfortunately, dishonest people rule the world. Good luck leading a happy life, and we hope you will read one of our upcoming books, which will uncover more ignorance throughout America.

Good luck with your life! I need a beer!

References and favorite sites (in no particular order):

The Fox News Channel	www.foxnews.com
The Neal Boortz Show	www.boortz.com
The Sean Hannity Show	www.hannity.com
The Bill O'Reilly Show	www.foxnews.com/oreilly
Citizens against Government Waste	www.cagw.org
The Media Research Center	www.mrc.org
NewsMax	www.newsmax.com
The Advocates	www.theadvocates.org
Townhall.com	www.townhall.com
The Drudge Report	www.drudge.com
The CIA Factbook	www.cia.gov/cia/publications/factbook
Fairtax.org	www.fairtax.org
Libertarian Party	www.lp.org
World Net Daily	www.worldnetdaily.com
The Heritage Foundation	www.heritage.org
National Center for Policy Analysis	www.ncpa.org

A lifelong love of research has gone into this book including, the Bible, the U.S. Constitution, the Declaration of Independence, and many others. A special mention to *History of the World*, volumes 1 & 2, by Bonanza Books and Crown Publishers, edited by Esmond Wright (Emeritus Professor of American History University of London).

978-0-595-36520-3
0-595-36520-5